behind APARTMENTS

A moment in the sublime ethics of Sūrat al-Hujurāt

Ahmed Hammuda

Cover design by Ahmad Chaker Jomaa

Edited by Ayshah Syed. Contact: ayshah.syed@outlook.com.

Ahmed Hammuda
For comments, feedback or constructive criticism, feel free to contact author:
ahmedhammuda@hotmail.com

Printed in the United Kingdom

First Printing: Aug 2020
Self-Published using Kindle Direct Publishing – Amazon

ISBN – 9798666775042

"The character of the Prophet of Allāh (sall Allāhu 'alayhi wa sallam) was the Qur'ān."

— 'Ā'ISHAH (*RAḌIY ALLĀHU 'ANHA*)

To my beloved mother and father, who nurtured us on Islām and taught us its sublime ethics

CONTENTS

ACKNOWLEDGEMENTS

In the name of Allāh, Most Gracious, Most Merciful. After praising and thanking Allāh, I extend my heartfelt appreciation to my pivotal guides and supporters. This includes my wife, Nazira for her unconditional and continuous support and encouragement throughout the writing of this book. I add my teacher, *Ustādh* Asim Khan, whose classes inspired me to share this resource with others and whose reflections provided a source for much of this work.

I also thank my esteemed teachers; my uncle Sheikh (Dr.) Husni Hammuda, and my brother *Ustādh* Ali Hammuda who revised this book from cover to cover, advising, correcting and endorsing its ideas. May Allāh fill their lives and hereafter with happiness and success. I thank my beloved friend Ahmad Chaker Jomaa who, besides advising me and supporting this work, designed a delightful front cover for it.

I add to this list the committee of the University of Kingston Islāmic Society, particularly the then-President, brother Hamad Momin, and, of course, the cohort of students who insisted on inviting me to deliver a lecture series on *al-Ḥujurāt*, receiving my sheer inexperience and often disordered discussions with encouragement and engagement. A number of the most enthusiastic attendees assisted in formulating this work, editing it, writing reflections, introductions, and conclusions.

I also sincerely thank sister Ayshah Syed, who very rigorously and professionally edited this work, correcting and advising throughout. I have included her contact details on the inside cover for those looking for expert proof-reading or editing. May Allāh reward all contributors and recognise them for their sincerity and commitment to the Qur'ān. Āmīn.

FOREWORD

All praise is due to Allāh, the Lord of the Worlds. And may Allāh's peace and salutations be sent upon His final Messenger and select servant, Muḥammad ﷺ, the guider to the straight path. We witness that he delivered the message, dispensed his duty and guided us to the loftiest manners and ethics.

One of the most critical lessons needed for humanity at this period in time is embedded in *Sūrat al-Ḥujurāt*, the 49th chapter of the Qur'ān. It truly is a gold mine of morals, values and practical instructions as per what the ideal Muslim society looks like. The fact that it is comprised of merely eighteen verses makes it evident that its nation-reforming properties can only be unpacked by a thinker, articulate writer and committed student of knowledge.

Linking past with present, scripture and rationale, and classical Arabia with modern, Western paradigms; this is precisely what the author has achieved. It is apparent from the style, analysis and unique deductions that Ahmed Hammuda has made from *Sūrat al-Ḥujurāt* – the subject matter of this book – that not only has he rigorously researched the ins and outs of this chapter, but has lived with it throughout his life, having confined himself almost exclusively to its companionship from the day he put pen to paper, until he had written its very last word.

Muslims of the 21st century are looking for guidance, leadership and quality content that use revelation and our classical Islamic texts as beacons of light, illuminating the path ahead amidst our sophisticated context. Ahmed Hammuda has made a key contribution in this department which I believe will be instrumental in paving the way forward in the coming years for Western Muslims and those worldwide.

- Ali Hammuda

Senior Researcher and Lecturer – Muslim Research and Development Foundation (MRDF) – *30th July, 2020 corresponding 9th Dhul Hijjah, 1441*

INTRODUCTION – THE QUR'ĀN AND ITS IMPACT

All praise is due to Allāh, the One Who revealed the Book as a warner and provider of good news. It is Allāh's greatest and final revelation, the seal of His scriptures, revealed to the seal of the Messengers and their chief, Muḥammad b. ʿAbdullāh ﷺ, through the intermediary of Allāh's select Angel, on the mightiest night of the chosen month. May Allāh's peace and blessings be upon His final and exemplary Messenger, the greatest exegete of Allāh's words, through which his companions were guided to the ideal way of life.

When Saʿd b. Hishām b. ʿĀmir (raḍiy Allāhu ʿanhu) asked the mother of the believers, ʿĀ'ishah (raḍiy Allāhu ʿanhā), about the conduct of the Messenger of Allāh ﷺ, she knew well that any description would fall short of truly encompassing the superiority of his manners. The reply of our eloquent mother and daughter of the *ṣiddīq* was simple and powerful. She said:

> أَلستَ تَقرَأُ القُرآنَ. قُلتُ، بَلَى. قَالَت، فَإِنَّ خُلُقَ نَبِيِّ اللَّهِ صَلَّى اللَّهُ عَلَيهِ وَسَلَّمَ كَانَ القُرآنَ. قَالَ، فَهَمَمْتُ أَن أَقُومَ وَلَا أَسأَلَ أَحَدًا عَن شَيْءٍ حَتَّى أَمُوتَ
>
> *"'Do you not read the Qur'ān?' I said, 'Of course.' She said, 'The character of the Prophet of Allāh ﷺ was the Qur'ān.' Saʿd said, 'I wanted to get up and not ask about anything else until I died...'"*[1]

The Qur'ān is a spring that never ceases to give. It is a wholesome curriculum which provides its adherents with distinction amidst a world running after unsubstantial and subjective guidance, codes, and legislations. When approaching the Qur'ān, one must perceive it for what it is: a perpetual miracle and an inimitable wonder that, since its

[1] *Ṣaḥīḥ* Muslim on the authority of ʿĀ'ishah (raḍiy Allāhu ʿanhā)

revelation, has baffled the brightest minds and overwhelmed the most thorough manmade texts and systems. All other miracles have ceased to exist. The Prophet ﷺ says:

> مَا مِنَ الأَنْبِيَاءِ نَبِيٌّ إِلاَّ أُعْطِيَ مِنَ الآيَاتِ مَا مِثْلُهُ أُومِنَ أَوْ آمَنَ عَلَيْهِ الْبَشَرُ. وَإِنَّمَا كَانَ الَّذِي أُوتِيتُ وَحْيًا أَوْحَاهُ اللَّهُ إِلَيَّ فَأَرْجُو أَنِّي أَكْثَرُهُمْ تَابِعًا يَوْمَ الْقِيَامَةِ
>
> *"There was no prophet among the prophets but was given miracles through which people had security or belief, but what I was given was the Divine Inspiration (the Qur'ān) which Allāh revealed to me. As such, I hope that my followers will be more than those of any other prophet on the Day of Resurrection."*[2]

The Qur'ān is the Muslim's share of these divine signs and miracles, one that remains fully accessible and available to us today. The Qur'ān was revealed in the age of poetry, during which civilisation experienced the pinnacle of linguistic eloquence. In pre-Islāmic Arabia men and women possessed such rhetoric proficiency that their words and expressions would outdo the hands of artists. They were people of piercing memory and oratory detail. Their powerful linguistic constructs were merged with profound wisdoms and insights. As such, poetry proliferated, catching on to day-to-day discourse, reshaping narratives, changing balances of power, creating reputations and destroying others. The strength of their poetry was such that it stood the test of time, and much of it is still preserved today.

It was precisely then that Allāh revealed His eternal challenge; a provocation specifically for those who proudly hung their impressive and distinctive literary pieces on the sanctified and oft-frequented Kaʿbah and for the world at large. Allāh's challenge also extended to the Jinn-kind whose literature was known and documented at the time. Allāh says:

> قُلْ لَئِنِ اجْتَمَعَتِ الْإِنْسُ وَالْجِنُّ عَلَى أَنْ يَأْتُوا بِمِثْلِ هَذَا الْقُرْآنِ لَا يَأْتُونَ بِمِثْلِهِ وَلَوْ كَانَ بَعْضُهُمْ لِبَعْضٍ ظَهِيرًا
>
> *Say, "If both men and Jinn banded together to produce the like of this Qur'ān, they could never produce anything like it, even if they backed each other up."*[3]

---

[2] *Ṣaḥīḥ* al-Bukhārī on the authority of Abū Hurairah (raḍiy Allāhu ʿanhu)

[3] Al-Qur'ān 17:88

The Qur'ān's unparalleled linguistic style does not come at the expense of its overwhelming depth or power to guide and reform. Its verses penetrated hardened hearts, minds, and consciences. Jubair b. Muṭʿim (raḍiy Allāhu ʿanhu), one of the leaders of the Quraish and a scholar in genealogy, said:

> سمعت النبي صلى الله عليه وسلم يقرأ في المغرب بالطور. فلما بلغ هذه الآية، أَمْ خُلِقُوا مِنْ غَيْرِ شَيْءٍ أَمْ هُمُ الْخَالِقُونَ ◊ أَمْ خَلَقُوا السَّمَوَاتِ وَالْأَرْضَ بَلْ لَا يُوقِنُونَ ◊ أَمْ عِنْدَهُمْ خَزَائِنُ رَبِّكَ أَمْ هُمُ الْمُصَيْطِرُونَ، كاد قلبي أن يطير
>
> *"I heard the Prophet ﷺ reciting Sūrah al-Ṭūr in the Maghrib prayer, and when he reached the verse, 'Or were they created out of nothing, or are they the creators? Or did they create the Heavens and the Earth? No, in truth they have no certainty. Or do they possess the treasuries of your Lord or do they have control of them? Or have they been given the authority to do as they like?'[4] My heart was about to fly out of its place."[5]*

During the early stages of the Da'wah, the Quraish elected one of its leaders, 'Utbah b. Rabīah, to negotiate with the Prophet ﷺ in the hopes of bringing an end to what they perceived as a threat to their social and economic fabric. 'Utbah visited the Prophet ﷺ and said:

> *"You have put your people in great trouble; you have created divisions among them; you consider them to be fools; you talk ill of their religion and gods ... if by what you are doing, you want wealth, we will give you enough of it so that you will be the richest man among us, if you want power, we will make you our chief and will never decide a matter without you."*

When he was done with his plea, the attentive and patient Prophet ﷺ replied with serenity and composure:

---

[4] Al-Qur'ān 52:35-37

[5] *Ṣaḥīḥ* al-Bukhārī on the authority of Jubair b. Muṭʿim (raḍiy Allāhu ʿanhu)

> بسم الله الرحمن الرحيم – حم ◊ تَنْزِيلٌ مِنَ الرَّحْمَنِ الرَّحِيمِ ◊ كِتَابٌ فُصِّلَتْ آيَاتُهُ قُرْآنًا عَرَبِيًّا لِقَوْمٍ
> يَعْلَمُونَ ◊ بَشِيرًا وَنَذِيرًا فَأَعْرَضَ أَكْثَرُهُمْ فَهُمْ لَا يَسْمَعُونَ ◊ وَقَالُوا قُلُوبُنَا فِي أَكِنَّةٍ مِمَّا تَدْعُونَا إِلَيْهِ
> وَفِي آذَانِنَا وَقْرٌ وَمِنْ بَيْنِنَا وَبَيْنِكَ حِجَابٌ فَاعْمَلْ إِنَّنَا عَامِلُونَ
>
> *"In the name of Allāh, the All-Merciful, the Most Merciful. Ḥā Mīm. A revelation from the All-Merciful, the Most Merciful. A Book whose verses have been demarcated for people who know as an Arabic Qur'ān, bringing good news and giving warning; but most of them have turned away and do not hear. They say, 'Our hearts are covered up against what you call us to and there is heaviness in our ears. There is a screen between us and you. So, act – we are certainly acting (meaning we will not change our ways).'"*[6]

'Utbah reclined on his hands listening. When the Prophet ﷺ reached the verse of prostration and prostrated 'Utbah got up and left without a question or objection. The Prophet ﷺ had recited the pure and unadulterated Qur'ān to a recipient who possessed unquestionable Arabic comprehension and eloquence without adding a word of commentary or analysis. The Prophet ﷺ knew it was something 'Utbah had never heard before, for it was directly from Allāh, and it left him bewildered, unsettled and changed.

Although he could not bring himself to admit it, his face and demeanour exposed his sentiments such that, upon seeing him, 'Utbah's clansmen asked one another, *"What happened? He looks entirely different to when he set off."* Then, in what was to become one of the most articulate and poignant expressions about the Qur'ān, 'Utbah replied:

> *"By Allāh I heard what I have never heard the likes of before. By Allāh it is not poetry nor is it sorcery nor is it magic. People of Quraish, listen to me and make me responsible [for my position]. Leave this man be, because by Allāh what he says will have serious effects [in the future]. If the other Arabs overcome him, you will be saved from having participated in fighting your brother and others will deal with him. But if he prevails over Arabia, his sovereignty will inevitably be your sovereignty and his honour your honour." They said, "You have been bewitched Abu al-Walīd."*[7]

---

[6] Al-Qur'ān 41:1-5

[7] Prophetic *Sīrah* – Ibn Hishām

The Qur'ān's impact reverberated throughout the world. It shook the hearts of educated Christian clergymen well-versed in divine scripture and expression. For them, it was not only confirmation of what they knew, but it had the familiar hallmark of divine speech that moved them to tears. Allāh says:

> وَإِذَا سَمِعُوا مَا أُنْزِلَ إِلَى الرَّسُولِ تَرَى أَعْيُنَهُمْ تَفِيضُ مِنَ الدَّمْعِ مِمَّا عَرَفُوا مِنَ الْحَقِّ يَقُولُونَ رَبَّنَا آمَنَّا فَاكْتُبْنَا مَعَ الشَّاهِدِينَ
>
> *When they listen to what has been sent down to the Messenger, you see their eyes overflowing with tears because of what they recognise of the truth. They say, "Our Lord, we have Īmān! So, write us down among the witnesses."*[8]

Beyond the perceived physical realm, the Qur'ān penetrated the heartlands of the hidden Jinn-kind who were bewildered by its meanings and presentation and were transformed, embracing Allāh's final religion. Allāh says:

> قُلْ أُوحِيَ إِلَيَّ أَنَّهُ اسْتَمَعَ نَفَرٌ مِنَ الْجِنِّ فَقَالُوا إِنَّا سَمِعْنَا قُرْآنًا عَجَبًا ۞ يَهْدِي إِلَى الرُّشْدِ فَآمَنَّا بِهِ وَلَنْ نُشْرِكَ بِرَبِّنَا أَحَدًا
>
> *Say, "It has been revealed to me that a band of the Jinn listened and said, 'We have heard a most amazing recitation (Qur'ān). It leads to right guidance so we believed in it and will not associate anyone with our Lord.'"*

Up until the Jinn said:

> وَأَنَّهُ كَانَ يَقُولُ سَفِيهُنَا عَلَى اللَّهِ شَطَطًا
>
> *"The foolish among us (i.e. Iblīs) used to utter vile slanders against Allāh."*[9]

Its truth was simply irresistible. After a single instance listening to the Prophet's recitation, whatever obedience and servitude they may have had for their master Iblīs were obliterated and they boldly declared the malice of Iblīs.

[8] Al-Qur'ān 5:83
[9] Al-Qur'ān 72:4

Perhaps more extraordinary still is the intense impact the Qur'ān had on the Angels. Despite their closeness to its source; their knowledge and direct interactions with transcendent realities, and their leader Jibrīl (ʿalayhi al-Salām) being the one to deliver it to the heart of the Messenger ﷺ, they were still taken aback by the magnificence of the Qur'ān.

Usaid b. Ḥuḍair (raḍiy Allāhu ʿanhu) reports that whilst he was reciting *Sūrat al-Baqarah* at night, his horse tied beside him began to act troubled. When he stopped reciting, his horse settled. When he started reciting again, the horse was startled again. Again, he stopped reciting and the horse settled. Usaid, afraid that his young son Yaḥyā who was sitting beside the horse would be trampled, ended his recitation. The next morning, he informed the Prophet ﷺ of his experience. The Prophet ﷺ was delighted, exclaiming:

> اقْرَأْ يَا ابْنَ حُضَيْرٍ. اقرأ يا بن حضير. قال، فأشفقتُ يا رسول الله أن تطأ يحيى وكان منها قريبًا. فرفعتُ رأسي فانصرفتُ إليه، فرفعتُ رأسي إلى السماء فإذا مثلُ الظلة فيها أمثالُ المصابيحِ فخرجتُ حتى لا أراها
>
> *"Recite, Ibn Hudair! Recite, Ibn Hudair!" He said, "Messenger of Allāh! My son Yaḥyā was near the horse and I was afraid that it might trample him. When I looked towards the sky and went to him, I saw something like a cloud containing what looked like lamps, so I left in order not to see it."*

The Prophet ﷺ said:

> وتدري ما ذاك؟ قال، لا. قال، تلك الملائكةُ دنَت لصوتِك، ولو قرأتَ لأصبحتْ ينظرُ الناسُ إليها لا تتوارى منهم
>
> *"Do you know what that was?" Ibn Hudair replied, "No." The Prophet ﷺ said, "Those were Angels who came near you for your voice and if you had kept on reciting until dawn, it would have remained there until the morning when people would have seen it and it would not have disappeared."*[10]

[10] *Ṣaḥīḥ* al-Bukhārī on the authority of Usaid b. Hudair (raḍiy Allāhu ʿanhu)

Exposure to the Qur'ān forged the most illustrious scholars, thinkers, and righteous men and women even from those who were otherwise headed for ruin. Imām Al-Dhahabī relates that the esteemed scholar of Islām al-Fuḍayl b. ʿIyād had taken to banditry in his youth, raiding caravans and robbing travellers. It was around this time he fell in love with a young girl and, on one occasion, decided to climb up the wall of her house. As he climbed, he overheard a voice reciting:

> أَلَمْ يَأْنِ لِلَّذِينَ آمَنُوا أَن تَخْشَعَ قُلُوبُهُمْ لِذِكْرِ اللَّهِ وَمَا نَزَلَ مِنَ الْحَقِّ وَلَا يَكُونُوا كَالَّذِينَ أُوتُوا الْكِتَابَ مِن قَبْلُ فَطَالَ عَلَيْهِمُ الْأَمَدُ فَقَسَتْ قُلُوبُهُمْ ۖ وَكَثِيرٌ مِّنْهُمْ فَاسِقُونَ
>
> *"Has the time not arrived for the hearts of those who have Īmān to yield to the remembrance of Allāh and to the truth He has sent down, so they are not like those who were given the Book before for whom the time seemed over long so that their hearts became hard? Many of them are deviators."*[11]

The verse jolted his heart and rejuvenated his dampened spiritual conscience. In one breath he said, *"Yes Allāh, now is the time!"* A single verse sparked the beginning of his admired journey of worship and scholarship, leading him to become one of the greatest Imāms of Islām and contributors to its rich heritage.

The Qur'ān not only transforms but distinguishes. The norms of social class, distinction, and recognition became all but redundant. Qur'ānic distinction would eclipse social hierarchies forever.

A man called Nāfiʿ b. ʿAbd al-Hārith met ʿUmar (raḍiy Allāhu ʿanhu) at a place called ʿUsfān. ʿUmar had employed Nāfiʿ as deputy over Makkah. In their meeting, ʿUmar asked Nafiʿ, *"Who did you appoint as deputy over the people of the valley [during your absence]?"* Nafiʿ replied, *"Ibn Abza."* ʿUmar asked, *"Who is Ibn Abza?"* Nafiʿ replied, *"He is one of our freed slaves."* ʿUmar asked, *"So you have appointed a freed slave over them?"* Nafiʿ said, *"He is well-versed in the Book of Allāh (ʿazza wa jal) and he is well-versed in the commandments and injunctions."* On hearing this, ʿUmar said:

> أَمَا إِنَّ نَبِيَّكُمْ صلى الله عليه وسلم قَدْ قَالَ، إِنَّ اللَّهَ يَرْفَعُ بِهَذَا الْكِتَابِ أَقْوَامًا وَيَضَعُ بِهِ آخَرِينَ

[11] Al-Qur'ān 57:16

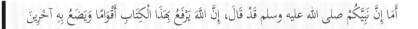

> *"Indeed, your Prophet ﷺ said, 'Through this Book, Allāh raises some and degrades others.'"*[12]

Notice the words *'your* Prophet' which would immediately dispel any objection that might arise. The one best acquainted with the Qur'ān is worthy of assuming leadership over Islām's holiest city, even if they once held the social status of a slave! This is but one of many examples in Islām's elaborate history.

In fact, the Qur'ān revived a civilisation that was virtually dead. The 600-year lull in heavenly revelation since the Abrahamic message of Jesus (ʿalayhi al-Salām) left much of humanity entirely lost for guidance. Just as the world lurked in darkness and disarray, seemingly destined for Hell, it found itself heading to Paradise. Just as it sunk into depression, misery, misguidance and loneliness, it was reintroduced to its purpose and Lord, for Whose closeness our hearts were created. From darkness, humanity began to see unblemished realities and developed a clear and vibrant picture of exactly where we are going and how to get there. Humanity was thus salvaged by Allāh's guidance, delivered entirely by His favour and grace (*Mann*).[13] Allāh says:

> لَقَد مَنَّ اللَّهُ عَلَى المُؤمِنينَ إِذ بَعَثَ فيهِم رَسولًا مِن أَنفُسِهِم يَتلو عَلَيهِم آياتِهِ وَيُزَكّيهِم وَيُعَلِّمُهُمُ الكِتابَ وَالحِكمَةَ وَإِن كانوا مِن قَبلُ لَفي ضَلالٍ مُبينٍ
>
> *Allāh showed great kindness (manna) to the believers when He sent a Messenger to them from among themselves to recite His Signs to them and purify them and teach them the Book and Wisdom, even though before that they were clearly misguided.*[14]

Nothing is more worthy of our time than Allāh's Book, for life is futile and meaningless without it. In the same way, nothing is worse than our detaching from it because by that we would be detaching our life from its very essence, bringing true death upon ourselves before the defunction of limbs. Undeniably, to throw away the purpose of our existence is to cease to exist at all.

To be gifted the Qur'ān means we are never truly deprived if we are rejected or suffer material loss. In the Qur'ān, after highlighting the rejection of the Makkan pagans, Allāh comforts our Prophet ﷺ. His is an experience common to previous prophets who sought to guide communities enmeshed in customary misguidance. In

---

[12] *Ṣaḥīḥ* Muslim on the authority of ʿAmir b. Wāthila (raḍiy Allāhu ʿanhu)

[13] Further explored in Section 2: Allāh's Great Favour, p. 74

[14] Al-Qur'ān 3:164

the subsequent verse, Allāh goes further still, reminding the Prophet ﷺ of the ultimate relief – that neither the distresses of rejection nor the sweetness of a message accepted compare to the gift of the Qur'ān:

> وَلَقَدْ آتَيْنَاكَ سَبْعًا مِّنَ الْمَثَانِي وَالْقُرْآنَ الْعَظِيمَ
>
> *We have given you the Seven Oft-repeated (meaning al-Fātiḥa) and the Magnificent Qur'ān.*[15]

In the verse that immediately follows, Allāh instructs the Prophet ﷺ:

> لَا تَمُدَّنَّ عَيْنَيْكَ إِلَىٰ مَا مَتَّعْنَا بِهِ أَزْوَاجًا مِّنْهُمْ وَلَا تَحْزَنْ عَلَيْهِمْ وَاخْفِضْ جَنَاحَكَ لِلْمُؤْمِنِينَ
>
> *Do not direct your eyes longingly to what We have given certain of them to enjoy. Do not feel sad concerning them. And take the believers under your wing.*[16]

Let us embark, then, on our journey through *al-Ḥujurāt* with the certitude that it will encompass some of the best advice we will ever receive. It is the literal word of Allāh (ʿazza wa jal) to which we should stand to attention and humble ourselves in awe and eager anticipation; it should shape our entire perspective. And all praise and thanks are due to Allāh.

---

[15] Al-Qur'ān 15:87
[16] Al-Qur'ān 15:88

AN OVERVIEW OF TAFSĪR

We spoke of the Qur'ān, the distinction of its people, its inimitability and far-reaching impact on its seekers. This leads us to one of its 114 chapters – *al-Ḥujurāt*. The forthcoming study of each of its sections will briefly contain what is known as *Tafsīr* and will conclude with *Tadabbur*.

Tafsīr can be loosely translated as: exegesis, interpretation, or clarification, and is both a process and result (verb and noun). Lingustically, the word comes from the Arabic word '*Fassara*', meaning *exposition* (*Kashf*) and *clarification* (*Bayān*). Thus, it is to clarify the explicit and intended meanings of the Qur'ān as per the interpreter or compiler's best ability. It is arrived at using the various tools and sciences surrounding the study of the Qur'ān. According to Badr al-Dīn al-Zarkashī:

> *"[Tafsīr is] A science through which the Book of Allāh, revealed upon His Prophet Muḥammad ﷺ, is understood, its meanings clarified, and its rulings and wisdoms derived" using the various sciences that underpin this endeavour, including "language, grammar, syntax, articulation (Balāghah), Islamic Fiqh, recitations, reasons for revelation, and the science of abrogation."*[17]

Tadabbur is typically translated as: reflection, derivation, or contemplation. It comes from the word '*Dubura*' meaning the end of something. The end, naturally, implies that there must be something available to begin with from which to derive an end. It is thus looking to the implication of a *Tafsīr* including the personal and societal implications of a verse. Thus, if *Tafsīr* is to understand the intended meaning, *Tadabbur* is to reflect on that meaning and its implications in order to increase one's Īmān, acquire beneficial knowledge and carry out good action.

The process of *Tafsīr* is laborious and involves having mastered the large collection of sciences that underpin reaching the intended meanings of the Qur'ān. Having

---

[17] *Al-Burhān fī 'Ulūm al-Qur'ān* – Badr al-Dīn al-Zarkashī

acquired and understood these basic meanings as a requisite, the exercise of *Tadabbur* becomes not only encouraged but imperative on everyone. As its hyperbolised Arabic form suggests, it also entails concerted effort and mental exercise. *Tadabbur* is, in fact, the *purpose* of the Qur'ān's revelation:

> كِتَابٌ أَنزَلْنَاهُ إِلَيْكَ مُبَارَكٌ لِّيَدَّبَّرُوا آيَاتِهِ وَلِيَتَذَكَّرَ أُولُو الْأَلْبَابِ
>
> *It is a Book We have sent down to you, full of blessing, so let people of intelligence ponder its Signs and take heed.*[18]

Allāh furthermore rebukes the hypocrites in Madīnah who, having understood the meanings of the Qur'ān which was revealed in their language, failed to consider its inimitability, authority, or carry out its implications:

> أَفَلَا يَتَدَبَّرُونَ الْقُرْآنَ ۚ وَلَوْ كَانَ مِنْ عِندِ غَيْرِ اللَّهِ لَوَجَدُوا فِيهِ اخْتِلَافًا كَثِيرًا
>
> *Will they not ponder the Qur'ān? If it had been from other than Allāh, they would have found many inconsistencies in it.*[19]

Considering the above definition of *Tafsīr*, it must be noted that the literal Qur'ānic text revealed upon the Messenger ﷺ is the unadulterated Arabic Qur'ān. Translators of the Qur'ān have followed the same process of exegesis to arrive at their translations. As such, these translations should be considered *Tafsīr* rather than non-Arabic renderings of Allāh's revealed Book. In this series, we have relied primarily on the priceless English translation of Aisha Bewley.

By Allāh's will, this book will relay the *Tafsīr* of the Qur'ān as is already available in some of the renowned books of *Tafsīr*.[20] It will separate out reasons for revelation and then delve into some *Tadabbur*.[21] This upcoming section is by no means exhaustive, but comprises the bulk of this book.

---

[18] Al-Qur'ān 38:29

[19] Al-Qur'ān 4:82

[20] Cf. *Jāmiʿ al-Bayān fī Ta'wīl al-Qur'ān* – Imām al-Ṭabarī; *Taysīr al-Karīm al-Raḥmān fī Tafsīr Kalām al-Mannān* – ʿAbdur-Raḥmān Al-Saʿdī; *Tafsīr al-Taḥrīr wa al-Tanwīr* – Ibn ʿĀshūr; *Al-Jāmiʿ li Aḥkām al-Qur'ān* – Imām Qurṭubī; *Tafsīr al-Qur'ān al-ʿAẓīm* – Ibn Kathīr, and *Tafsīr of al-Ḥujurāt* by Sheikh Muḥammad al-Shaʿrāwī (and others)

[21] These will be sourced from the authors of the aforementioned books of *Tafsīr*, extracted from their works, or derived at as a result of further contemplation.

Revising our Intentions

Let us take a moment to revise our intentions. Intentions are dynamic and challenging to perfect. Each believer will have their own method of perfecting their intentions. Irrespective of the technique used, it must be a recurrent and dedicated effort, revisiting the worthy intentions that are often drowned out by social gatherings, preoccupations with reputation, or the desire for approval.

Time and effort are better dedicated towards what will last. Imagine devoting years compiling a piece of work only to desire a moment of transient human recognition. Then on the Day of Resurrection, you find those who recognised you wanting nothing but their own salvation, even if at your own expense! As such, we should strive to intend:

- **To seek the Face of Allāh** and to earn His pleasure. This endeavour is a token of our appreciation of His Book and final revelation. In this we show Him gratitude and hope that He will look at us spending our time studying His words and attempting to understand His guidance to the best of our ability.

- **To become better slaves and worshippers of Allāh** by immediately implementing what we learn into our lives and among our families, in particular the ethics and manners delivered in this chapter as we recognise this as its purpose before the study of its linguistic nuances and implied meanings.

- **After removing our own ignorance, to then assume it our responsibility to share** Allāh's words with the rest of the world, seeking to address the ignorance of others and guide them in order to reform society.

The Qur'ān is about studying collectively as there is more barakah – blessing and benefit in doing that. It is traditionally taught through *Mudārasah* – a two-way learning process which aims to create a dialogue. Admittedly, this is challenging to achieve through the medium of a book. The reader, however, can use some of the ideas and reflections presented to open the floor for contributions when teaching them to others. An attempt has been made to prompt thought and questions where possible, with some answers provided.

This study will attempt to alternate between technical or basic legalistic theory, practical application, and heart-softening reminders, if Allāh wills. We will present the meanings of verses and explore further dimensions including the wider context of these meanings; how they relate to one another; some of the implied and subtle messages; further reflections on these meanings, and ways to apply them in our lives. These tools and techniques will, by Allāh's leave, help us achieve our three primary intentions outlined above. And Allāh is the source of strength.

A THEMATIC DISCUSSION

A*l-Ḥujurāt* is the 49th chapter of the Qur'ān. Thematically, it is said to be centred on:

> التربية الأخلاقية للأمة الإسلامية
>
> *"Nurturing the behaviour of the Muslim Ummah."*[22]

Although it speaks of general behaviours and ethics, the essential caveat is that these values can only be embraced and realised with the prerequisite *Īmān*; a wholesome term comprising inner cognisance and conviction, verbal validation of that conviction, and its manifestation through action. In English texts, *Īmān* is often translated as belief and those who have *Īmān* as believers. Clearly, this rendering is restrictive and misrepresents the comprehensiveness of the term. Thus, if English references are made to *belief* or *believers* in place of the Arabic *Īmān* or *Mu'minūn*, the reader is encouraged to recall the more nuanced definition of this vital designation.

Many of the ethics directed by *al-Ḥujurāt* can only be appreciated with *Īmān*. Consider, first of all, that societies lacking in *Īmān* defy physical, outer regulation as a concept,[23] and thus, naturally, elide dogmatic regulation of their inner selves as well. And now consider that *al-Ḥujurāt*'s outer ethics are inextricably linked to inner presuppositions and regulations. Without *Īmān*, most will only regulate their manners in the presence of others, in conformance to perceived societal sensibilities or as

---

[22] *Al-Tarbiyah al-Akhlāqiyyah fī Sūrat al-Ḥujurāt* – Dr. Abdusalam Hamdan al-Lawh – Gaza

[23] Hence the emergence of modern liberalist thought from a secular (counter-*Īmāni*) starting point.

subjects to the law *if* the law can 'see' them. Unless one is conscious of Allāh – who is ever-watchful over our hearts and secrets – why would one assume ethics *in secret*?

Similarly, a person who rejects Allāh altogether, or Muḥammad ﷺ, will most assuredly not put them both ahead of their own ideas and beliefs, which is the first instruction and premise of *al-Ḥujurāt*'s ethics. Therefore, we can state that the main theme of *Sūrat al-Ḥujurāt* is to nurture and perfect the mannerisms of believers (*Mu'minūn*).

In this chapter alone, Allāh addresses the believers through *'You who have Īmān'* (*yā ayyuha alladhīna āmanū*) **five** times. On only one occasion He addresses all people generally with 'Mankind' (*yā ayyuha al-nās*) in conjunction with the concept of God-consciousness (*Taqwā*). *Taqwā* is the deep cognisance of God which encourages good action and prevents one from doing evil. The level of *Taqwā* represents a person's honour by Allāh's measurement. Disclosure of the ultimate benchmark of selection and distinction known as *Taqwā* must be expressed to every human being, irrespective of whether they are *Mu'min* or *Kāfir* and irrespective of creed, colour or nationality.

Sūrat al-Ḥujurāt pays particular emphasis on the perfection of characteristics and manners towards the Messenger of Allāh ﷺ, as well as between one another, both in one another's presence and in one another's absence. It speaks of such manners in times of reconciliation and peace; in times of dispute and argumentation, and with those 'less practicing' or possessing lower levels of *Īmān*.[24] In each of these circumstances, Allāh reminds us of His ultimate awareness of the most secret matters and thoughts hidden in and among people's hearts and subtle actions. *Al-Ḥujurāt*, therefore, addresses mannerisms towards:

> *1 - Allāh*
> *2 - His Messenger*
> *3 - The Fussāq (rebellious, deviants or sinners)*[25]
> *4 - The present believer*
> *5 - The absent believer*

Each interaction above is preceded and introduced with *'yā ayyuha alladhīna āmanū'*.[26] We will discuss how each individual section of the *Sūrah* serves its overall theme or purpose. 'Perfecting' good manners must make provision for dispelling their opposite, namely, the characteristics that some had retained from their days of pre-Islāmic ignorance (*Jāhiliyyah*). The bad manners of the Jāhiliyyah included:

---

[24] Further explored in Section 2: Who is a Fāsiq? p. 65
[25] Ibid., p. 65
[26] *Tafsīr al-Taḥrīr wa al-Tanwīr* – Ibn ʿĀshūr

1 - Harshness
2 - Bluntness
3 - Hearsay
4 - Argumentation
5 - Mockery
6 - Evil suspicion
7 - Spying
8 - Backbiting
9 - Showing off
10 - Counting one's favours on their recipient (Mann)

Each one of these bad manners is individually remedied by *al-Ḥujurāt*, reinstating them with upright ethics brought by the pure religion of Islām that had spread throughout the precincts of Arabia. Such remedies and ethics are imperative for each and every one of us on our journey to Allāh and the Hereafter.

Subjects of Al-Ḥujurāt

Our journey through *al-Ḥujurāt* will consist of a multidimensional study with relation to the wider context of the meanings of the *Sūrah*, how they relate to one another, the implied messages, applications and reflections. With the tools of Tafsīr and Tadabbur, we can elucidate and apply the central theme of the *Sūrah*. Later we will explore the intricateness of the style, structure, and content of the *Sūrah*, highlighting how its name and structural features are all assimilated and connected.

For the sake of structuring this text and facilitating both learning and delivery, we will go by a suggestive sectioning of the *Sūrah* into the following five parts:[27]

1 - Mannerisms with Allāh and His Messenger ﷺ, verses 1-5
2 - Verifying news and obeying righteous leadership, verses 6-8
3 - Conflict resolution and reconciling between Muslims, verses 9-10
4 - A general collection of manners and ethics, verses 11-13
5 - The reality of Īmān in Allāh, verses 14-18

[27] *Al-Tarbiyah al-Akhlāqiyyah fī Sūrat al-Ḥujurāt* – Dr. Abdusalam Hamdan al-Lawh – Gaza

The Meanings of its Name

The *Sūrah* is only known by the name *'al-Ḥujurāt'*. Unlike many other chapters in the Qur'ān, the vast majority – if not all – of the scholars of Tafsīr (*Mufassirūn*) refer to it by this name. Later exegetes such as Ibn ʿĀshūr and others report a consensus on this.

The term *'Ḥujurāt'* specifically refers to the apartments of the Prophet's wives. There were nine of them in total, built around the Prophet's Masjid and separated with palm leaf stalks. Most were situated on the eastern side of the now green carpeted Rawdah. Since Makkah sits to the south of Madīnah, the *Ḥujrah* (singular of *Ḥujurāt*) of ʿĀ'ishah (raḍiy Allāhu ʿanha) in which our beloved Messenger ﷺ is buried, is positioned to the worshipper's left when facing the Qiblah. Each Ḥujrah was originally a small, squared room, with a ceiling around 2.5m high and with a door that led directly into the Masjid of the Prophet ﷺ.

Connecting the Name with the Theme

The fact that the *Sūrah* has only this name indicates that it is one that is restricted and regulated (*Tawqīfi*), accepting no suggestive change. In all likelihood, it reflects Prophetic stipulation – consensus usually does. With this in mind, the name deserves a pause and some reflection. Why is a *Sūrah* that primarily addresses mannerisms named "The Prophet's Apartments"? This discussion does not escape the best efforts of deduction and is by no means exhaustive or absolute. However, returning to the root of the word and referencing its occurrence in the actual *Sūrah* may give us a good indication of the association. Allāh says:

> إِنَّ ٱلَّذِينَ يُنَادُونَكَ مِن وَرَاءِ ٱلْحُجُرَاتِ أَكْثَرُهُمْ لَا يَعْقِلُونَ
>
> *As for those who call out to you from outside your private quarters, most of them do not use their intellect.*[28]

We already appreciate that the main message of this *Sūrah* is to perfect character with Allāh, His Messenger and with one another. A precondition to the perfection of that character is to acknowledge and accept the position of Allāh and His Messenger; this is to exhibit sound Īmān and Taqwā. Those who called out the Messenger ﷺ were a group of Bedouins from the tribe Banī Tamīm.[29] They had gathered around the

---

[28] Al-Qur'ān 49:4

[29] Further explored in Section 1: Those who called out the Messenger, p. 51

Ḥujurāt of the Prophet ﷺ, raising their voices and making statements unbefitting of him and his due veneration. They behaved out of character.

To tie this behaviour with the name, it is necessary to return to the name's Arabic origin. Though *Ḥujurāt* refers specifically to the apartments of the wives of the Prophet ﷺ, it comes from the trilateral root *Ḥa Ja Ra*. This root word literally means: to prevent or to seclude, usually a piece of land using bricks or stone in order to demarcate it or to bar access.

The name of the *Sūrah*, therefore, suggests that in their careless treatment of the Prophet ﷺ, their hearts exhibited the hardness of stone used to build the *Ḥujurāt*. In English, *hard-heartedness* is used to highlight a cold brashness, and emotional or spiritual indifference. As for the Bedouins, their hard-heartedness barred their hearts from engaging in better comportment befitting the eminence of he whom they addressed: the Prophet ﷺ. Recall what Allāh says regarding the hearts of some of the Banī Isrā'īl:

> ثُمَّ قَسَت قُلوبُكُم مِن بَعدِ ذٰلِكَ فَهِيَ كَالحِجارَةِ أَو أَشَدُّ قَسوَةً ۚ وَإِنَّ مِنَ الحِجارَةِ لَما يَتَفَجَّرُ مِنهُ
> الأَنهارُ ۚ وَإِنَّ مِنها لَما يَشَّقَّقُ فَيَخرُجُ مِنهُ الماءُ ۚ وَإِنَّ مِنها لَما يَهبِطُ مِن خَشيَةِ اللَّهِ ۗ وَمَا اللَّهُ بِغافِلٍ
> عَمّا تَعمَلونَ
>
> *Then your hearts became hardened after that, so they were like rocks (Ḥijārah) or even harder still. There are some rocks from which rivers gush out, and others which split open and water pours out, and others which crash down from fear of Allāh. Allāh is not unaware of what you do.*[30]

There is an inseparable correlation between their limited experience with the Messenger of Allāh ﷺ, or their newness to Islām, and their engagement in the bad manners alluded to earlier. Harshness, bluntness, argumentation, and backbiting had been fostered by their hardened, indifferent hearts. Their hearts were *prevented* (*taḥajjarat*) from emotionally and spiritually softening to his eminence and presence ﷺ, and correspondingly to the inviolability of their siblings in Islām. The name *al-Ḥujurāt* revokes the humanity of those who do not appropriately revere the Prophet ﷺ by likening them to the inanimate stone.[31,32] This is yet another interconnection between the name of the *Sūrah* and its namesake substance.

---

[30] Al-Qur'ān 2:74

[31] *Maḥāsin al-Ta'wīl* – al-Qāsimi

[32] *Al-Tarbiyah al-Akhlāqiyyah fī Sūrat al-Ḥujurāt* – Dr. Abdusalam Hamdan al-Lawh – Gaza

TIME OF REVELATION

There is more or less agreement that *al-Ḥujurāt* was revealed in the Madani era. A minority of scholars have suggested that verse 13 (concerning *Taqwā*) was revealed before the Hijrah. Others have attempted to reconcile this difference by stating that verse 13 was revealed in Makkah but after the conquest of Makkah. Thus, the verse could be Makki by way of *where* it was revealed, but Madani by its nature.

Expounding briefly on this, every verse revealed after the Hijrah can be considered Madani regardless of where it was physically revealed. Scholars of Tafsīr thus reason that the differentiation of Makki and Madani is based on time of revelation, rather than place of revelation. More precisely, the *Sūrah* was revealed in what is known as the Year of the Delegates (*'Ām al-Wufūd*) in the 9th year of the Hijrah, and is therefore one of the last chapters of the Qur'ān to be revealed.

An obvious question poses itself here. People have been Muslim for a long period of time and *al-Ḥujurāt*, without doubt, covers certain matters pertaining to this reality. But how is it that certain rudimentary manners and ethics are being discussed in the very latter part of the Sīrah? Surely many instructions in the Qur'ān had already been revealed and implemented; did the companions need such elementary character building?

To answer this question, one must first explore the Year of the Delegates. During this phase of the Sīrah it had been several years since the Battle of the Trench (*al-Khandaq*) during which Muslims had repelled an Arab-wide coalition against Madīnah. Makkah was likewise conquered, and the Muslims had recently returned from the Expedition of Tabūk in which the Roman superpower failed to turn up and put up a fight. The Arabs surrounding Madīnah were naturally in awe of the Prophetic community. It had now established itself as the power bloc of Arabia, fearless in the face of the empires the Arabs had traditionally cowered before. By Allāh's grace, political ties began to turn in favour of the Muslims.

Naturally, many tribes began sending delegations to the Prophet ﷺ, renouncing their traditional beliefs and embracing the religion of Allāh in droves. Many, however, still carried pre-Islāmic tendencies and ignorant habits. Many had only accepted Islām because of its new political dominance, while others did so for other motives. *Al-Ḥujurāt* would cultivate true Īmān in the hearts of this new cohort of Muslims and nurture their character (*Akhlāq*) to fall in line with the teachings of Islām, and as embodied by the earliest Mu'minūn.

Link to Surrounding Chapters

The ordering of the Qur'ān is not haphazard. It is divinely inspired and full of wisdom. Let us take a moment to contemplate the placement of *al-Ḥujurāt*. Towards the end of *Sūrat al-Fatḥ*, the 48th chapter placed before *al-Ḥujurāt*, Allāh says:

> مُّحَمَّدٌ رَّسُولُ اللَّهِ ۚ وَالَّذِينَ مَعَهُ أَشِدَّاءُ عَلَى الْكُفَّارِ رُحَمَاءُ بَيْنَهُمْ ۖ تَرَاهُمْ رُكَّعًا سُجَّدًا يَبْتَغُونَ فَضْلًا مِّنَ اللَّهِ وَرِضْوَانًا
>
> *Muḥammad is the Messenger of Allāh, and those who are with him are fierce to the disbelievers, merciful to one another. You see them bowing and prostrating, seeking Allāh's good favour and His pleasure.*[33]

Just before the commencement of *al-Ḥujurāt*, we find that Allāh praises the Holy Prophet ﷺ and those with him who supported him and his cause. Accordingly, the beginning of *al-Ḥujurāt* outlines the sublime manners due to Allāh and the Prophet ﷺ that will enable the Muslim populace, or '*those who have Īmān*' (*alladhīna āmanū*), to resemble that category mentioned at the end of *al-Fatḥ*.[34] In fact, *al-Ḥujurāt* contrasts the behaviour of Islām's new entrants with the companions outlined at the end of *al-Fatḥ* providing them with the role-models to emulate.

What then is the connection between *al-Ḥujurāt* and Chapter 50, '*Qāf*'? Consider the last verse of *al-Ḥujurāt*:

> إِنَّ اللَّهَ يَعْلَمُ غَيْبَ السَّمَاوَاتِ وَالْأَرْضِ ۚ وَاللَّهُ بَصِيرٌ بِمَا تَعْمَلُونَ
>
> *Allāh knows the* ***unseen things*** *of the Heavens and the Earth. Allāh sees what you do.*[35]

In a demonstration of perfect harmony, *Qāf* then begins with '*Qāf*', one of the Qur'ān's separated letters (*al-Ḥurūf al-Muqaṭa'ah*), the definitive and full meanings of which are reserved with Allāh. That is, their elaborate meanings are of the *unseen things* (*Ghayb*) that emphasise man's limited knowledge.

---

[33] Al-Qur'ān 48:29

[34] *Al-Tarbiyah al-Akhlāqiyyah fī Surat al-Ḥujurāt* – Dr. Abdusalam Hamdan al-Lawh – Gaza

[35] Al-Qur'ān 49:18

How, then, do the themes of the two chapters of *al-Ḥujurāt* and *Qāf* compare? Revisit *Qāf* and find it focuses on the terrifying episodes of the Day of Reckoning. Allāh says:

> وَجاءَت سَكرَةُ المَوتِ بِالحَقِّ ۖ ذٰلِكَ ما كُنتَ مِنهُ تَحيدُ
>
> *The throes of death come revealing the truth. That is what you were trying to evade!*[36]
>
> وَنُفِخَ فِي الصّورِ ۚ ذٰلِكَ يَومُ الوَعيدِ
>
> *The Trumpet will be blown. That is the Day of the Threat.*[37]
>
> وَجاءَت كُلُّ نَفسٍ مَعَها سائِقٌ وَشَهيدٌ
>
> *Every self will come together with a driver and a witness.*[38]
>
> لَقَد كُنتَ في غَفلَةٍ مِن هٰذا فَكَشَفنا عَنكَ غِطاءَكَ فَبَصَرُكَ اليَومَ حَديدٌ
>
> *You were heedless of this so We have stripped you of your covering and today your sight is sharp.*[39]

Until Allāh says:

> يَومَ نَقولُ لِجَهَنَّمَ هَلِ امتَلَأتِ وَتَقولُ هَل مِن مَزيدٍ
>
> *On the Day He says to Hell, "Are you full?" it will ask, "Are there no more to come?"*[40]

If *al-Ḥujurāt* is centred on the importance of good manners, or the encouragement and enticement (*Targhīb*) towards embracing them, *Qāf* is centred on the severe repercussions (*Tarhīb*) of their negligence. *Qāf* underlines that neglectful behaviour towards Allāh, His Messenger, and the believers is a serious matter as there are punishing and horrifying days ahead of us. It is on that Day that we will, most assuredly, see the fruits of our manners and actions.

---

[36] Al-Qur'ān 50:19
[37] Al-Qur'ān 50:20
[38] Al-Qur'ān 50:21
[39] Al-Qur'ān 50:22
[40] Al-Qur'ān 50:30

The Beginning and the End

Of note is that the first verse begins by mentioning the knowledge of Allāh:

> ...وَاتَّقُوا اللَّهَ ۚ إِنَّ اللَّهَ سَمِيعٌ عَلِيمٌ
>
> *... and have Taqwā of Allāh. Allāh is All-Hearing, All-Knowing.*[41]

And likewise, the last verse of *al-Ḥujurāt* outlines the all-encompassing knowledge of Allāh:

> إِنَّ اللَّهَ يَعْلَمُ غَيْبَ السَّمَاوَاتِ وَالْأَرْضِ ۚ وَاللَّهُ بَصِيرٌ بِمَا تَعْمَلُونَ
>
> *Allāh **knows the unseen** things of the Heavens and the Earth. Allāh **sees what you do**.*[42]

The chapter is therefore bracketed between two reminders of Allāh's knowledge. The latter of which is of His knowledge of the open and the secret, which is the greatest threat for those mentioned in the former; those who put themselves forward of Allāh and His Messenger ﷺ, even in their inner dimension.[43]

The fact that the *Sūrah* is encapsulated in Allāh's knowledge should come as no surprise as it is full of commandments. Submitting to commandments, without doubt, is taxing. The opposite is also true. Self-serving behaviours such as gossip are easy, and even entertaining. Backbiting and ostracising others, too, create the feeling of dominance and favourability. Mistreating others is easier than sacrificing or *restraining* our tongues in pursuit of their comfort and reputation. It is difficult to honour our seniors and challenging to lower our voices, particularly when the propensity to make our opinions heard makes us loud and entitled. Preserving the reputation of others in their presence and absence is trying enough.

What then can be said about regulating our *inward* thoughts and suspicions? A person may question why they should carry such a heavy burden. The answer is because it is borne out of Allāh's divine knowledge and infallible legislation. Allāh *knows*, undoubtedly, that these instructions will benefit rather than stifle us. And a load that will definitely benefit us is a load worth bearing.

---

[41] Al-Qur'ān 49:1

[42] Al-Qur'ān 49:18

[43] *Nathm al-Durar fī tanāsub al-Suwar* – al-Biqā'ī

'You who have Īmān' coupled with the command to 'do such and such' contains a call that anticipates a person's response based on their Īmān. Your proactivity or, conversely, your hesitation or resentment towards obeying illustrates your level of Īmān. May Allāh increase our Īmān.

49

THE IMPORTANCE OF *AL-ḤUJURĀT*'S GENERAL MESSAGE

Humans are natured upon loving good character. A person of great character is the recognised master of their community. No religion has delved into the importance of great manners more than Islām, the religion of the natural disposition (*Fitrah*). The uniqueness of Islām, moreover, is that it has firmly tied mannerisms to eternal salvation, as well as emphasising their worldly benefits. Nothing improves a person's morality and ethics quite like believing in accountability after death or to have Īmān.

Let us consider, for example, that a gesture of good happens to bring a person *no* satisfaction, *no* financial reward, and *no* appreciation. Consider if the recipient of your gesture is an orphan, too young to thank you and even less likely to pay you back, with no parents to do so on their behalf. A Mu'min will hope for Allāh's recognition in the afterlife, even if it never comes from the vulnerable recipient, and thus persevere for them, never rebuffing them, because of their Īmān. With this perspective, revisit the oft-recited versės in which Allāh says:

> أَرَأَيْتَ الَّذِي يُكَذِّبُ بِالدِّينِ
>
> *Have you seen him who denies the recompense [in the Last Day]?*
>
> فَذَٰلِكَ الَّذِي يَدُعُّ الْيَتِيمَ
>
> *He is the one who harshly rebuffs the orphan...*[44]

Al-Ḥujurāt's general message, as discussed in **'A Thematic Discussion'**, is to nurture the behaviour of the Muslim Ummah. It begins with the necessity of revering Allāh and His Prophet and appreciating the social structure of a Muslim civilisation. This becomes the premise for what follows – *objectively* verifying news; obeying leadership; dispelling differences; resolving conflict, and reconciling between believers. The *Sūrah* thus becomes almost an embellishment of the verse in another chapter:

> يَا أَيُّهَا الَّذِينَ آمَنُوا أَطِيعُوا اللَّهَ وَأَطِيعُوا الرَّسُولَ وَأُولِي الْأَمْرِ مِنكُمْ ۖ فَإِن تَنَازَعْتُمْ فِي شَيْءٍ فَرُدُّوهُ إِلَى
> اللَّهِ وَالرَّسُولِ إِن كُنتُمْ تُؤْمِنُونَ بِاللَّهِ وَالْيَوْمِ الْآخِرِ ۚ ذَٰلِكَ خَيْرٌ وَأَحْسَنُ تَأْوِيلًا

[44] Al-Qur'ān 107:1-2

> *You who have Īmān!* ***Obey Allāh and obey the Messenger and those in command among you.*** *If you have a dispute about something, refer it back to Allāh and the Messenger, if you have Īmān in Allāh and the Last Day. That is the best thing to do and gives the best result.*[45]

The *Sūrah* then extrapolates on general etiquettes and mannerisms, many of which concern the hidden dimension, such as suspicion, back-biting and spying. Most conflicts occur by revealing unseen matters, such as suspecting the worst, spying on what was otherwise hidden, and revealing what was otherwise unknown to others. However, this *Sūrah* emphasises that knowledge of such unseen matters must be returned to Allāh and can never stand as a basis for judgement.

"Nations are Manners, So Long as They Remain"[46]

Al-Ḥujurāt's mannerisms are timeless, and it is through them that Islām prevailed across the globe. Oppressive empires barred the message from reaching their subjects, but with the sacrifice of Islām's adherents, who fought and toiled, the message took charge, giving those same subjects the choice of entering the fold. It led nations by example and attracted scores of others to accept that sublime way of life.

Supreme manners, besides other exclusivities, are the hallmark of Islāmic empires. Many Muslim nations were, in fact, created without a fight, including the largest present-day nations of East Asia. Despite being archetypically known for their excellent social ethics (before Islām), they embraced Islām after being impressed by the superior ethics exhibited by the companions. One could only imagine what they saw. Many have thus associated this *Sūrah* with building the Muslim civilisation. Its message can be understood beyond the individual level to a global political one.

Internal strife and conflict that bring down a nation, after first separating families and friends, begin with either the *external* misbehaviour of either party or due to *internal* blemished ideas and suspicions about one another. All the while, conflict is exacerbated when the concept of Islāmic brotherhood (*Ukhuwwah*) is undermined. *Al-Ḥujurāt* unpicks every one of these issues, one after the other, and in so doing fortifies families, friends, the community and nations. The Egyptian poet Aḥmed Shawqī famously said:

إنما الأمَمُ الأخْلاقُ ما بَقِيَتْ   فإِنْ هُمُ ذَهَبَتْ أخْلاقُهُم ذَهَبُواْ

[45] Al-Qur'ān 4:59
[46] Egyptian poet - Aḥmed Shawqī

"Nations are nothing but manners, so long as they remain. If their manners depart, so too will those nations."

Your Manners are Perceived as Islām

According to the Syrian scholar Prof. Moḥammed Rāteb al-Nabulsi, the Muslim in the Muslim world is recognised as an individual. His ill manners fall against his individuality, exclusively by name. In the West, however, the Muslim is perceived as Islām itself, irrespective of how much we try to emphasise the separation between *Islām* and *Muslims*. One's colleagues have not read the Qur'ān or Sunnah, nor are they likely to read the Sīrah. *You* are the manifestation of Islām as far as they are concerned. For one, manners speak much louder than words. And as the representatives of Islām in the West, this is both a considerable burden but also a huge opportunity.

Consider a cloudy and rainy Sunday afternoon. A lonely student sits in their tiny apartment asking themselves if there is more to life than this materialistic rat race. His or her disposition is finally knocking on their conscience. Suddenly, they get a message on their phone. It is a video of Muslims brawling, or fighting with the police. They are left saying, *"I would never do anything like that and I am not even religious."* This is one of the connotations of Allāh's words:

> رَبَّنَا لَا تَجْعَلْنَا فِتْنَةً لِّلَّذِينَ كَفَرُوا وَاغْفِرْ لَنَا رَبَّنَا ۖ إِنَّكَ أَنتَ الْعَزِيزُ الْحَكِيمُ
>
> *"Our Lord!* ***Make us not a trial for the disbelievers,*** *and forgive us, Our Lord! Verily, You, only You, are the All-Mighty, the All-Wise."*[47]

Through our poor conduct we become a trial for the non-Muslims. Our disgraceful circumstances assure them that by rejecting Islām they must be doing the right thing! In this respect, our actions fuel a fervent rejection of Īmān rather than a hungry inclination towards it.

Our separation of 'religiosity' and manners is, in fact, also becoming a fitnah for Muslims, particularly as some practicing Muslims become known for nothing but rigidness, argumentation, and refutation. I recall a beloved brother insisting I read a book about the deviances of a particular Sunni movement to which I asked, *"Do you instead have a book that can save me from Hell and enter me into Paradise?"* To his credit, he replied, *"You have none other than the Book of Allāh – the Qur'ān"* and gave a genuinely warm laugh.

---

[47] Al-Qur'ān 60:5

In our locality, a marriage between two practicing individuals was hampered after the brother refused to meet the father of the sister (her legal guardian – *waliy*) since he perceived him an innovator. Regardless of his incorrect assessment, imagine if that father was faint-hearted; what would become of his perception of practicing young brothers the next time they proposed? The Prophet ﷺ, in fact, makes *manners* one of two conditions women and their legal guardians should seek out in marriage, hand-in-hand with religiosity. He says:

> إِذَا خَطَبَ إِلَيْكُمْ مَنْ تَرْضَوْنَ دِينَهُ وَخُلُقَهُ فَزَوِّجُوهُ إِلاَّ تَفْعَلُوا تَكُنْ فِتْنَةٌ فِي الأَرْضِ وَفَسَادٌ عَرِيضٌ
>
> *"When someone whose religion and character you are pleased with proposes to [someone under the care] of one of you, then marry [her] to him. If you do not do so, then there will be turmoil (Fitnah) in the land and abounding discord (Fasād)."*[48]

Those who perceive *manners* and *religiosity* as separable play a contributory role in the fitnah that ensues from families electing to marry their daughters to non-practicing men who happen to be well-mannered, fearing the mercilessness and harshness of the opposite. But more importantly, what value do our prescribed acts of worship or our external attire carry if we behave without any Islamic regulation? The Prophet ﷺ said:

> مَا شَيْءٌ أَثْقَلُ فِي مِيزَانِ الْمُؤْمِنِ يَوْمَ الْقِيَامَةِ مِنْ خُلُقٍ حَسَنٍ وَإِنَّ اللَّهَ لَيُبْغِضُ الْفَاحِشَ الْبَذِيءَ
>
> *"Nothing is heavier on the believer's scale on the Day of Judgement than good character. For indeed Allāh, Most High, is angered by the shameless obscene person."*[49]

And he said:

> إِنَّ مِنْ أَحَبِّكُمْ إِلَيَّ وَأَقْرَبِكُمْ مِنِّي مَجْلِسًا يَوْمَ الْقِيَامَةِ أَحَاسِنَكُمْ أَخْلاَقًا

---

[48] Al-Tirmidhī and Ibn Mājah on the authority of Abu Hurairah (raḍiy Allāhu ʿanhu)
[49] Al-Tirmidhī on the authority of Abu ad-Dardā' (raḍiy Allāhu ʿanhu)

> *"The most beloved among you to me, and the nearest to sit with me on the Day of Judgement, is the best of you in character."*[50]

And he said:

> إِنَّ الرجلَ لَيُدْرِكُ بحسنِ خُلُقِهِ دَرَجَاتِ قائِمِ الليلِ، صائِمِ النَّهارِ
>
> *"A believer will reach through good manners the rank of one who prays during the night and observes fasting during the day."*[51]

By Allāh's permission we will extrapolate further on this in later parts. All praise and thanks are due to Allāh alone.

[50] Al-Tirmidhī on the authority of Jābir b. ʿAbdullāh (raḍiy Allāhu ʿanhu)
[51] Abu Dāwūd on the ʿĀ'ishah (raḍiy Allāhu ʿanhā)

SECTION 1: MANNERS WITH ALLĀH AND HIS MESSENGER

After laying the foundations of *al-Ḥujurāt*, touching on its thematic message, meticulous placement, and structure, let us shed light on the first of its five parts. This is the noblest and most rudimentary mannerism on which all objectively upright conduct and behaviour is founded. It is a call directed at those of Īmān concerning how a person should behave with Allāh and His Messenger ﷺ, instructing them not to put their speech or actions ahead of them. It advises that our own preferences, opinions, and actions are secondary to those decreed by Allāh and His Messenger ﷺ. Those of Īmān recognise that the Messenger ﷺ says nothing out of his own accord, but is the conveyor of Allāh's will and decree. Allāh says:

> وَمَا يَنطِقُ عَنِ الْهَوَىٰ ۞ إِنْ هُوَ إِلَّا وَحْيٌ يُوحَىٰ
>
> *Nor does he speak from whim. It is nothing but Revelation revealed.*[52]

[52] Al-Qur'ān 53:3-4

Verses 1-5

> بِسْمِ اللَّهِ الرَّحْمَٰنِ الرَّحِيمِ – يا أَيُّهَا الَّذِينَ آمَنوا لا تُقَدِّموا بَينَ يَدَيِ اللَّهِ وَرَسولِهِ ۖ وَاتَّقُوا اللَّهَ ۚ إِنَّ اللَّهَ سَميعٌ عَليمٌ ◊ يا أَيُّهَا الَّذينَ آمَنوا لا تَرفَعوا أَصواتَكُم فَوقَ صَوتِ النَّبِيِّ وَلا تَجهَروا لَهُ بِالقَولِ كَجَهرِ بَعضِكُم لِبَعضٍ أَن تَحبَطَ أَعمالُكُم وَأَنتُم لا تَشعُرونَ ◊ إِنَّ الَّذينَ يَغُضّونَ أَصواتَهُم عِندَ رَسولِ اللَّهِ أُولٰئِكَ الَّذينَ امتَحَنَ اللَّهُ قُلوبَهُم لِلتَّقوىٰ ۚ لَهُم مَغفِرَةٌ وَأَجرٌ عَظيمٌ ◊ إِنَّ الَّذينَ يُنادونَكَ مِن وَراءِ الحُجُراتِ أَكثَرُهُم لا يَعقِلونَ ◊ وَلَو أَنَّهُم صَبَروا حَتّىٰ تَخرُجَ إِلَيهِم لَكانَ خَيرًا لَهُم ۚ وَاللَّهُ غَفورٌ رَحيمٌ
>
> *You who have Īmān! Do not put yourselves forward in front of Allāh and of His Messenger; and have Taqwā of Allāh. Allāh is All-Hearing, All-Knowing. You who have Īmān! Do not raise your voices above the voice of the Prophet and do not be as loud when speaking to him as you are when speaking to one another, lest your actions should come to nothing without your realising it. Those who lower their voices when they are with the Messenger of Allāh are people whose hearts Allāh has tested for Taqwā. They will have forgiveness and an immense reward. As for those who call out to you from outside your private quarters, most of them do not use their intellect. If they had only been patient until you came out to them, it would have been better for them. But Allāh is Ever-Forgiving, Most Merciful.*[53]

Verse 1:

Allāh introduces *al-Ḥujurāt* with:

> يا أَيُّهَا الَّذينَ آمَنوا لا تُقَدِّموا بَينَ يَدَيِ اللَّهِ وَرَسولِهِ ۖ وَاتَّقُوا اللَّهَ ۚ إِنَّ اللَّهَ سَميعٌ عَليمٌ

[53] Al-Qur'ān 49:1-4

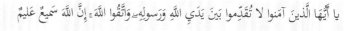

> *You who have Īmān! Do not put yourselves forward in front of Allāh and of His Messenger, and have Taqwā of Allāh. Allāh is All-Hearing, All-Knowing.*[54]

The verse is understood as follows:

'You who have testified to the Oneness of Allāh and the Prophethood of Muḥammad ﷺ, do not hasten in a matter involving your military or religious affairs before Allāh and His Messenger issue their own decree. In doing so you may decide in a manner contrary to what Allāh and His Messenger have decided. And have fear of Allāh in your hearts that you may be protected from saying what Allāh and His Messenger have not permitted in any of your affairs. And be cognisant of Allāh, because Allāh hears what you say and knows well what you intend by your speech. Nothing is hidden from Him, not even your innermost thoughts.'[55]

The judicious student of Tafsīr will notice how in this concise statement, Imām al-Ṭabarī (d. 310AH) collects and harmonises many of the earliest opinions. His distinction in this approach has earnt his work the title *"The Mother of all Tafāsīr"*. This is notwithstanding the fact that many of the succeeding compilations based their works on the compilations and derivations of al-Ṭabarī. In this particular verse, he brings together no less than five transmissions (singular. *Riwāyah*) sourced from the earliest Qur'ānic exegetes (*Mufassirūn*), carrying out an analysis (*Dirāyah*) of these texts to produce an amicable conclusion.

To exemplify this, Ibn ʿAbbās (raḍiy Allāhu ʿanhu) expounds on the verse by saying, *"Do not say what is contrary to the Qur'ān and Sunnah."* Mujāhid, a student of Ibn ʿAbbās, says, *"Do not precede the Prophet ﷺ in [proclaiming] anything until Allāh decrees it on his tongue [first]."* Qatādah explains it by way of providing an example, adding, *"Some people used to say 'if only such and such was revealed, then such and such a ruling would no longer apply.'"* Thus, the instruction was to counter such sentiments. Al-Ḥasan al-Baṣrī relates that some people rushed to sacrifice their sacrificial animal (*Uḍḥiyah*) before the Prophet ﷺ had sacrificed his own. Others like al-Ḍaḥāk indicate that the verse refers specifically to matters of war, in which there were those who opined in a manner contrary to that of the Prophet ﷺ.[56]

Primarily, these scholarly opinions are different ways of expressing the same meaning, or illustrative examples sourced from the same meaning. This is what is known in the science of Tafsīr as complimentary differences of opinion (*Ikhtilāf al-Tanawwu'*). In the realm of the earliest Tafsīr, this is the most common form of

[54] Al-Qur'ān 49:1
[55] *Jāmiʿ al-Bayān fī Ta'wīl al-Qur'ān* – Imām al-Ṭabarī
[56] *Jāmiʿ al-Bayān fī Ta'wīl al-Qur'ān* – Imām al-Ṭabarī

difference and is conciliatory in nature as it is of no real difference.[57] Imām al-Ṭabarī commonly weaves together all such opinions when presenting his Tafsīr, only giving preference of one opinion over another when they cannot be reconciled. With this in mind, the verse *'Do not put yourselves ahead of Allāh and His Messenger'* can be understood as a prohibition of putting one's self, whether in wants or opinions, before Allāh and His Messenger in *absolutely any matter*.

'You who have Īmān!' (*Yā ayyuha alladhīna āmanū*) creates anticipation on the part of the receiver. The characteristic identifier used of those *'who have Īmān'* gives the listener an admirable and valued identity making them more likely to obey the instruction that follows.[58] The heart of the recipient is softened and prepared for the upcoming firm reminder, addressing the defiant nature of man when presented with reprimand or advice.

'Put yourselves forward' (*tuqaddimū* or *tataqaddamū*) depicts one physically walking in front of the Messenger and leaving him behind.[59] The physical manifestation of the prohibition impacts the recipient of this warning with its gravity.

Linguistically, the *object* (*Maf'ūl*) is excluded. The Arabic can literally be rendered as 'do not put... ahead of Allāh and His Messenger'. Notice that no particular 'thing' is specified. This omission has the interesting effect of encapsulating *anything* and *everything*.[60] It is almost as if to say, 'do not put ... *anything of your choosing*, whether an opinion, a statement, or an action, ahead of what Allāh and His Messenger have already directed,' for the Prophet's ﷺ will is in harmony with Allāh's.

The prohibition here does not necessarily imply that anyone in the Prophetic community necessarily put themselves forward of Allāh or His Messenger. It is only by way of warning. Moreover, it applies if it is possible to ascertain the Prophet's ﷺ decree in the first place. If such is not available, then one's best judgement based on objective knowledge and effort can be exercised.

Obedience: Absolute vs. Conditional

It should be noted that obedience is, in general, either *absolute* or *conditional*. This meaning is demonstrated in the wording of the verse previously quoted:

يَا أَيُّهَا الَّذِينَ آمَنُوا أَطِيعُوا اللَّهَ وَأَطِيعُوا الرَّسُولَ وَأُولِي الْأَمْرِ مِنكُمْ

---

[57] *Al-Muqqadimah fī Usūl al-Tafsīr* – Ibn Taymiyyah
[58] *Tafsīr al-Taḥrīr wa al-Tanwīr* – Ibn 'Āshūr
[59] *Tafsīr al-Taḥrīr wa al-Tanwīr* – Ibn 'Āshūr
[60] *Fatḥ al-Qadīr* – al-Shawkāni

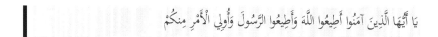

> *You who have Īmān! Obey Allāh and obey the Messenger and those in command among you.*[61]

Notice that, unlike the absolute obedience afforded to Allāh and His Messenger ﷺ through the repeated command 'obey', the instruction to the third group (*'those in command among you'*) was not preceded with 'obey'. The linguistic implication being the obedience afforded to this latter group, either those in political authority or otherwise, is necessary but *conditional* upon their own obedience to Allāh and His Messenger when dispensing their authority. The obedience is thus an Islamically legal type (*Shar'ī*) in anything other than sin, not the tyrannical type (*Tāghutī*),[62] that compels obedience, irrespective of the nature of the directive.

Those in command cannot be obeyed if they command what displeases Allāh and His Messenger ﷺ, as their authority stems from them through Islām. In much the same way, following them in what does please Allāh is part of obeying Allāh Himself. In recent times, this reality has become totally distorted by many living under absolutist regimes dressed with religious attire. Obedience to the fallible *ruler* (*waliyyul 'amr*) can never be absolute, as prioritising their directives to sin means putting them before Allāh and His Messenger ﷺ. Islām came to affirm one form of *absolute* servitude and to abolish the rest. The primary role of the *waliyyul 'amr* is to reflect Allāh's will on Earth, not to deform it in favour of his own throne, territory or cause of injustice. The verse before the aforementioned (of *al-Nisā'*) aptly states:

> إِنَّ اللَّهَ يَأْمُرُكُم أَن تُؤَدُّوا الأَماناتِ إِلىٰ أَهلِها وَإِذا حَكَمتُم بَينَ النّاسِ أَن تَحكُموا بِالعَدلِ ۚ إِنَّ اللَّهَ
> نِعِمّا يَعِظُكُم بِهِ ۗ إِنَّ اللَّهَ كانَ سَميعًا بَصيرًا
>
> *Allāh commands you to* ***return to their owners the things you hold on trust*** *and, when you judge between people, to* ***judge with justice****. How excellent is what Allāh exhorts you to do! Allāh is All-Hearing, All-Seeing.*[63]

After commanding that rights be returned to their owners in verse 58 of *al-Nisā'*, is it conceivable that verse 59 of *al-Nisā'* be interpreted as commanding obedience to the squanderers of trusts and advocates of injustice? The Prophet ﷺ says:

---

[61] Al-Qur'ān 4:59
[62] See *Fatḥ al-Qadīr* – al-Shawkāni
[63] Al-Qur'ān 4:58

> على المرء المسلم السمع والطاعة فيما أحب وكره، إلا أن يؤمر بمعصية، فإذا أمر بمعصية فلا سمع ولا طاعة
>
> *"It is obligatory upon a Muslim to listen [to the ruler] and obey whether he likes it or not, except when he is ordered to do a sinful thing. In such a case, there is no obligation to listen or to obey."*[64]

Abu Bakr's (raḍiy Allāhu ʿanhu) words in his first ascent to the eminent pulpit of *Khilāfah* immediately after the Messenger ﷺ were:

> أطيعوني ما أطعت الله ورسوله، فإذا عصيت الله ورسوله فلا طاعة لي عليكم
>
> *"Obey me, so long as I obey Allāh and His Messenger. And should I stop obeying Allāh and His Messenger, that requirement of obedience towards me is no longer."*[65]

It is therefore of the worst forms of deception and betrayal of trust for leaders to first go against Allāh's will on Earth, then employ their royal clergy to demand unconditional obedience, utilising decontextualised evidences related to obeying *worthy* leaders before slamming critics as heretics and *Khawārij*. Islām came to free people from the manacles and degradation of enslavement to men, to the unlimited expanse and empowerment of serving the Creator, individually and collectively. Every human after the Messenger of Allāh ﷺ is a subject under Allāh and His Messenger and exclusively accountable to Allāh:

> إِن كُلُّ مَن فِي السَّمَاوَاتِ وَالْأَرْضِ إِلَّا آتِي الرَّحْمَٰنِ عَبْدًا ◊ لَّقَدْ أَحْصَاهُمْ وَعَدَّهُمْ عَدًّا ◊ وَكُلُّهُمْ آتِيهِ يَوْمَ الْقِيَامَةِ فَرْدًا
>
> *There is no one in the Heavens and Earth who will not come to the All-Merciful as a slave. He has counted them and numbered them precisely. Each of them will come to Him on the Day of Rising all alone.*[66]

---

[64] *Ṣaḥīḥ* Bukhārī and Muslim on the authority of ʿAbdullāh b. ʿUmar (raḍiy Allāhu ʿanhu)
[65] Mentioned in *al-Bidāyah wa al-Nihāyah* with an authentic chain of transmission
[66] Al-Qur'ān 19:93-95

Divine Knowledge and Objective Personal Effort and Opinion

In his Tafsīr, Ibn Kathīr recalls when the Prophet ﷺ sent Muʿādh b. Jabal (raḍiy Allāhu ʿanhu) to the people of Yemen.[67] In his advice, he asked Muʿādh:

> *"How will you judge?" Muʿādh replied, "I will judge according to what is in Allāh's Book." The Prophet said, "If it is not in Allāh's Book?" Muʿādh replied, "Then with the Sunnah of the Messenger of Allāh ﷺ." The Prophet said, "If it is not in the Sunnah of Messenger of Allāh ﷺ?" Muʿādh replied, "I will give my view based on my best effort (Ijtihād)." He said:*
>
> الْحَمْدُ لِلَّهِ الَّذِي وَفَّقَ رسولَ رسولِ اللَّهِ، لِمَا يَرْضَى رَسُولُ اللَّهِ
>
> *"All praise is due to Allāh, the One Who guided the messenger of the Messenger of Allāh to that which pleases the Messenger of Allāh."*[68]

In this intense and wholesome narration, the prioritisation by Muʿādh is clear. The Qur'ān accompanied by the Sunnah clarifies absolutely all matters either explicitly or by derivation from the general objectives they set out. Where that guidance is explicit, it prevails over our own, notwithstanding the fact that our informed views and opinions have undeniable weight in areas which Islām has given leeway.

The process of legal reasoning (*Ijtihād*) is likewise not putting oneself forward (*Taqdīm*), as the person carrying it out (the *Mujtahid*) will try his best to work within the parameters of Islām. In the absence of definitive guidance, or in situations where accessibility to knowledge is scarce, a Muslim should be well acquainted with what Islām seeks out such as the preservation of faith, justice, fairness, chastity, life, sanity and health. Therefore, within these parameters, a Muslim can make a well-intentioned and objective decision, being truthful with themselves about what the right thing to do is, even if it contradicts their personal inclinations or comforts.

In reflecting on this section, let us actively nurture our hearts upon the belief that our Creator and Cherisher, Allāh, and His select Prophet and Messenger ﷺ know best. The measure of success is that we harbour no discomfort towards divine directives. And if we find ourselves longing that something was made *Ḥalāl* or another were *Ḥarām*, let us sit down with ourselves and tell our hearts again that the Creator Who

---

[67] *Tafsīr al-Qur'ān al-ʿAẓīm* – Ibn Kathīr

[68] Abu Dāwūd on the authority of 'some men who were companions of Muʿādh' as appears in the ḥadīth's transmission. There is a vast difference of opinion concerning the authenticity of this ḥadīth, but many scholars have accepted it and it has a number of corroborating reports that support it.

is '*All-Hearing, All-Knowing*' knows what is best for us. And all praise and thanks belong to Allāh alone.

THE MESSENGER IS LIKE NONE OTHER

In our introduction to the first section of *al-Ḥujurāt* which governs our manners with Allāh and His Messenger ﷺ, we explored how the *Sūrah* repeatedly appeals to our *Īmān*; a part of which is recognising the prominence and precedence of Allāh and His Messenger ﷺ. Once recognised, the call is repeated again and again to underpin the abundant mannerisms Allāh prescribes among the rest of creation.

In 1908, Ottoman ruler Sultan ʿAbdul Ḥamīd II inaugurated the nearly 1,500 km Hejaz railway, which connected Istanbul to the Hejaz, serving pilgrims to Makkah. An entire wagon was dedicated as a Masjid with a full-time caller to prayer (*Mu'adhin*). The journey between Damascus and Madīnah, which took 40 days on camel, was reduced to just 72 hours. In an intriguing display of ingenuity, engineers coated both the nails on the tracks approaching the Madīnah station and the trains' wheels with felt – a material made with compressed natural fibres.[69] This was to reduce the rumbling sound of the train in the Prophet's revered presence and to embody the following verse of *al-Ḥujurāt*:

Verse 2

> يا أَيُّهَا الَّذِينَ آمَنوا لا تَرفَعوا أَصواتَكُم فَوقَ صَوتِ النَّبِيِّ وَلا تَجهَروا لَهُ بِالقَولِ كَجَهرِ بَعضِكُم لِبَعضٍ أَن تَحبَطَ أَعمالُكُم وَأَنتُم لا تَشعُرونَ
>
> *You who have Īmān! Do not raise your voices above the voice of the Prophet and do not be as loud when speaking to him as you are when speaking to one another, lest your actions should come to nothing without your realising it.*[70]

The verse is understood as:

'You who have believed in Allāh and His Messenger, do not raise your voices above that of the Messenger of Allāh, speaking harshly to him or addressing him bluntly. Likewise, do not address him the same way you would address one another, using his plain name 'Muḥammad' instead of a respectable title such as 'Prophet of Allāh' or

---

[69] B., Ekrem, *"Hejaz railway: A historic line to Islām's holiest cities"*, Daily Sabah (Turkey, 28th October 2016)

[70] Al-Qur'ān 49:2

'Messenger of Allāh'. Raising your voices above that of your Prophet will render your actions obsolete, to no reward, without you even noticing.'[71]

Supporting this meaning, Allāh says in another verse:

> لَا تَجْعَلُوا دُعَاءَ الرَّسُولِ بَيْنَكُمْ كَدُعَاءِ بَعْضِكُم بَعْضًا
>
> *Do not make [your] calling of the Messenger among yourselves as the call of one of you to another.*[72]

This does not imply that if the Prophet ﷺ raises his voice, you are also licensed to raise yours, so long as it remains lower than his. Rather, one should not raise their voice in his presence above the ordinary and perceptible level. The verse, moreover, does not infer complete silence in his noble presence, nor prohibits the particular occasions the Prophet ﷺ requested his companions to raise their voices such as in warfare, raising the *Adhān*, and the like.[73]

Raising Your Voice – A Cause to Nullify Your Deeds

How can an instance of raising the voice above the Messenger ﷺ physically, or raising it symbolically above his purified Sunnah, render all of one's actions entirely obsolete? This question is particularly relevant when it is known that actions only become *entirely* obsolete when one leaves Islām in favour of disbelief (*Kufr*). Allāh says:

> وَمَن يَرْتَدِدْ مِنكُمْ عَن دِينِهِ فَيَمُتْ وَهُوَ كَافِرٌ فَأُولَٰئِكَ حَبِطَتْ أَعْمَالُهُمْ فِي الدُّنْيَا وَالْآخِرَةِ ۖ وَأُولَٰئِكَ
> أَصْحَابُ النَّارِ ۖ هُمْ فِيهَا خَالِدُونَ

[71] *Jāmi' al-Bayān fī Ta'wīl al-Qur'ān* – Imām al-Ṭabarī
[72] Al-Qur'ān 24:63
[73] *Tafsīr al-Taḥrīr wa al-Tanwīr* – Ibn 'Āshūr

> *As for any of you who revert from their Dīn and dies a Kāfir, their actions will come to nothing in this world and the Next World. They are the Companions of the Fire, remaining in it timelessly, for ever.*[74]

Where is the resemblance between the two? The short answer is that *contempt* of any degree is almost always the very first step to outright defiance and rejection. Have you ever wondered why 'Contempt of Court' in most countries is such a heinous offence? This is because it defies the core of legal authority, i.e., its authoritative, overriding nature, and shakes the necessary basis of the judiciary being above the rest. Relatedly, the Messenger ﷺ is Islām's definitive authority and, as such, worthier of such veneration. Thus, nothing should be put above him – neither voice nor action – or else the entirety of Islām's jurisdiction will be gradually eroded. Notice that Islām's antagonists target the character of the noble Messenger ﷺ for this very reason, for it is the easiest way to undermine *all of Islām.*

Ibn ʿAṭiyyah explains that raising one's voice can progressively develop religious detachment in the heart. If a person becomes accustomed to such, their convictions may continue to recede until they are led to Kufr,[75] or they may become set on intentional contempt – which is decidedly Kufr. It is thus that something we may see as trivial (one's spoken volume) develops into something far worse and leads to a gradual decline in one's veneration. Ibn ʿĀshūr adds:

> *"Repeatedly disrespecting the Prophet ﷺ will make one accustomed to such, until its continuity causes the Prophet's veneration to lessen in oneself ... until that person sees no need to show him respect at all and this is Kufr."*

The fact that this Kufr can occur *'without your realising'* is because whilst a person vividly recognises binary changes of religious state (from *Īmān* to *Kufr*), one hardly ever senses gradual diminishment. The verse could also be understood to mean that *some* of one's actions will diminish (the amount of which Allāh knows).[76]

The Messenger is Unique

Al-Ḥujurāt teaches us that the first and most paramount dimension of *ethical* development is to appreciate that the Messenger of Allāh ﷺ is unlike anyone else. Every person's directives and subjective understanding of ethics are open to being

---

[74] Al-Qur'ān 2:217

[75] *Al-Muharrar al-Wajīz* – Ibn ʿAṭiyyah

[76] *Tafsīr al-Taḥrīr wa al-Tanwīr* – Ibn ʿĀshūr

challenged, held to account, or disagreed with, except the Prophet ﷺ. ʿAbdullāh b. ʿAbbās (raḍiy Allāhu ʿanhu) is reported to have said:

> مَا أَحَدٌ مِنَ النَّاسِ إِلَّا يُؤْخَذُ مِنْ قَوْلِهِ وَيُدَعُ غَيْرَ النَّبِيِّ عَلَيْهِ الصَّلَاةُ وَالسَّلَامُ
>
> *"There are none except that you can take from their words or reject except the Prophet ﷺ."*[77]

He is the reference from whose mouth only emerges truth, and he is *infallible* insofar as the information he delivers about Allāh is concerned. As such, his actions and verdicts are naturally superior, and his status is unique and protected. His position with Allāh is unlike anyone or anything else and he is decisively Allāh's greatest slave and Messenger, ﷺ.

As such, no matter how much we try, we will fail to appreciate the true extent of his greatness. But an exploration of the following may bring us somewhat closer:

If you search the entire Qur'ān, you will notice that Allāh, the King of Kings, never addresses his Prophet Muḥammad ﷺ by his plain, direct name, such as to say *'yā* Muḥammad'. There is an abundance of examples of other prophets being addressed in this way such as, *'yā* Ādam',[78] *'yā* Nūḥ',[79] *'yā* Ibrāhīm',[80] *'yā* Mūsā',[81] and so on.[82] The addresses of *'yā'*, when used to address the Final Messenger are instead *always* associated with his characteristic or title. For example, *'yā ayuha al-Rasūl'* (O Messenger) and *'yā ayuha al-Nabī'* (O Prophet). If his Creator has given him such status and honour, addressing him *only* by his distinguished status and title, as He instructs in *al-Ḥujurāt*, who are we as his followers to afford him anything less?

Allāh praises his intellect, manners, heart, body, eyesight, reputation, companions, and household. His esteemed status is both in the explicit and subtle Qur'ānic discourse. Consider another fascinating and beautifully subtle inference to his unrivalled eminence in the Eyes of his Creator, *ʿazza wa jal*. When the Qur'ān discusses Mūsā (ʿalayhi al-Salām) being spoken to, Allāh uses this account as a testament to the truthfulness of the Qur'ān, as Muḥammad ﷺ did not witness the incident first hand, let alone report it. During the encounter, we know that Mūsā (ʿalayhi al-Salām) was standing on the *right-hand side* of the mountain when he was addressed by his Lord:

---

[77] Narrated by ʿAbdullāh b. Aḥmad in *Zawā'id al-Zuhd*

[78] Al-Qur'ān 2:35

[79] Al-Qur'ān 11:46

[80] Al-Qur'ān 11:76

[81] Al-Qur'ān 20:11

[82] *Tafsīr al-Ḥujurāt* – Muḥammad Metwalī al-Shaʿrāwī

> وَنَادَيْنَاهُ مِن جَانِبِ الطُّورِ الْأَيْمَنِ وَقَرَّبْنَاهُ نَجِيًّا
>
> *We called out to him from the right-hand side of the Mount and We brought him near in close communication.*[83]

Allāh proceeds by telling us that His beloved Messenger ﷺ was not on that side of the mountain to be able to relate the encounter from his own memory, but that it was inspired to him:

> وَمَا كُنتَ بِجَانِبِ الْغَرْبِيِّ إِذْ قَضَيْنَا إِلَىٰ مُوسَى الْأَمْرَ وَمَا كُنتَ مِنَ الشَّاهِدِينَ
>
> *You were not on the western side when We gave Mūsā the command. You were not a witness.*[84]

Focus on this subtlety. Rather than say, 'You were not on the *right side*', Allāh chooses to say, '*You were not on the western side*'. Such meticulous wording is in case it comes across as having denied the favoured '*right*' side from His Messenger ﷺ, or in case it gives the impression that the opposite is implied. The Prophet ﷺ was not positioned to the west of the mountain, but is forever on the *right side*.[85] It comes as no surprise that one's decibel level should not go above his, even as he rests silently in his purified grave.[86] The area of his grave is not one for chatter, selfies, pushing and shoving or other such misbehaviour. Instead, it should be a place of serenity, majesty, seriousness, and deliberation.

Your veneration of Allāh's chosen Messenger is tantamount to your veneration of Allāh Who selected him. And this is but a prelude to a whole host of manners and ethics that will build wholesome individuals, families, societies, and nations that are firmly bonded and perfectly structured. And Allāh is the source of strength.

---

[83] Al-Qur'ān 19:52
[84] Al-Qur'ān 28:44
[85] Mentioned to this effect in *Ta'amulāt Qur'āniyyah* – Ṣāliḥ al-Maghamsi
[86] *Al-Jāmi' li Aḥkām al-Qur'ān* – Imām Qurṭubī

LOWER YOUR VOICE IN THE PROPHET'S REVERED PRESENCE

Being in the majestic presence of the Prophet ﷺ is no minor privilege. He is *the greatest* of Allāh's creation to have existed and will ever exist. In a ḥadīth, he praised some who will come in later generations harbouring, *'the keenest desire to catch a glimpse of me even at the cost of his family and wealth.'*[87] If a *glimpse* in exchange of your possessions is the worthiest exchange, what can be said of the gravity of contempt? After touching on the severity of even unintentionally raising one's voice above that of the Messenger ﷺ, the address is relaxed. Allāh reassures the outstanding Prophetic community that the merit of the opposite conduct also holds true.

Verse 3

> إِنَّ الَّذِينَ يَغُضُّونَ أَصْوَاتَهُمْ عِندَ رَسُولِ اللَّهِ أُولَٰئِكَ الَّذِينَ امْتَحَنَ اللَّهُ قُلُوبَهُمْ لِلتَّقْوَىٰ ۚ لَهُم مَّغْفِرَةٌ وَأَجْرٌ عَظِيمٌ
>
> *Those who lower their voices when they are with the Messenger of Allāh are people whose hearts Allāh has tested for Taqwā. They will have forgiveness and an immense reward.*[88]

Those who hold back from raising their voices in the presence of the Messenger of Allāh ﷺ, addressing him with softness and politeness, are those whose hearts Allāh has tested by selecting them and purifying them for *Taqwā*. *Taqwā* is to carry out Allāh's obedience and to abstain from His disobedience. Such purification is much like the way gold is purified (*yumtaḥan*) with fire, removing its impurities (the ore) and keeping its essence. These people will be forgiven and overlooked their previous sins. They will be given the great reward of Paradise (*Jannah*).[89] 'Tested for *Taqwā*' can be understood as Allāh having purified their hearts such that they have become worthy and accommodating vessels for the excellent inner circumstance of Taqwā.

---

[87] *Ṣaḥīḥ* Muslim on the authority of Abu Hurairah (raḍiy Allāhu ʿanhu)
[88] Al-Qur'ān 49:3
[89] *Jāmiʿ al-Bayān fī Ta'wīl al-Qur'ān* – Imām al-Ṭabarī

'*Inna*' at the start of the verse is a rhetorical device used for emphasis (*Ḥarfu Ta'kīd*). The meaning is '*surely*', '*certainly*' and '*without doubt*'. 'They' (*ulā'ik*), on the other hand, is grammatically a demonstrative pronoun (*Ismu Ishāra*). You are being told to turn your attention, for *it is this* exemplary, illustrious and demonstrative category of people who are worthy of being mentioned.[90] Its positioning further favours them, so as to say that this noteworthy group, *besides all others*, are those whose hearts have been purified for Taqwā.

Verse 4

> إِنَّ الَّذِينَ يُنَادُونَكَ مِن وَرَاءِ الْحُجُرَاتِ أَكْثَرُهُمْ لَا يَعْقِلُونَ
>
> *As for those who call out to you from outside your private quarters, most of them do not use their intellect.*[91]

Now, addressing His Prophet ﷺ, Allāh states that most of those who call him from behind the apartments are ignorant (*juhāl*) in the religion of Allāh,[92] and in what the Prophet ﷺ deserves of dues and veneration.[93] This verse both clarifies the preceding directive ('*Do not be as loud when speaking to him as you are when speaking to one another*') and gives an example of those who broke it.[94]

To give you another glimpse into the remarkable and inimitable construct of the Qur'ān, notice how embedded within the fourth verse is the reason the previous verses (1-3) were revealed! Here, in the Qur'ān's unique style, it outlines the directive *before* the incident that begot that directive, without compromising understanding or clarity. The use of '*aktharuhum*' (most of them) is to exclude those who did not call out the Prophet ﷺ in the same way.[95]

---

[90] *Tafsīr al-Taḥrīr wa al-Tanwīr* – Ibn 'Āshūr

[91] Al-Qur'ān 49:4

[92] This verse and the one that follows were revealed concerning a group of people from a tribe of Bedouins called Banī Tamīm who came calling the Messenger from behind his apartments saying, "*Muḥammad, come out and meet us*". Further explored in Section 1: Those Who Called Out the Messenger, p. 51

[93] *Jāmi' al-Bayān fī Ta'wīl al-Qur'ān* – Imām al-Ṭabarī

[94] Al-Qur'ān 49:2

[95] *Tafsīr al-Taḥrīr wa al-Tanwīr* – Ibn 'Āshūr

Verse 5

> وَلَوْ أَنَّهُمْ صَبَرُوا حَتَّىٰ تَخْرُجَ إِلَيْهِمْ لَكَانَ خَيْرًا لَّهُمْ ۚ وَاللَّهُ غَفُورٌ رَّحِيمٌ
>
> *If they had only been patient until you came out to them, it would have been better for them. But Allāh is Ever-Forgiving, Most Merciful.*[96]

'If those who called you, O Muḥammad, from behind the apartments were patient such that they waited until you came out to them, rather than calling out to you, that would have been better for them in the sight of Allāh. This is as Allāh had ordered them to revere and honour you, but Allāh is Ever-Forgiving, Most Merciful. He will forgive those who called you out from behind the apartments, on condition they desist and repent, and will be Merciful towards them, never punishing them after their repentance.'[97]

This welcoming call from the Most-Gracious and Most-Merciful Lord is one that is likely to entice them towards seeking the forgiveness Allāh promises. According to Ibn ʿĀshūr, the wording in fact indicates that Allāh had already overlooked their incorrect behaviour, otherwise He would have explicitly requested their tawbah. Banī Tamīm, being part of Islām's newest cohort of Muslims, still had a lot to learn, and in many cases, ignorance can excuse a person from blame.[98] And Allāh knows best.

Who Taught You 'Good Action'?

In our previous discussion, we noted how raising one's voice above the Messenger ﷺ can render all good deeds obsolete. Though some may internally feel this is a disproportionate outcome for a 'minor' misdeed, it is, in fact, entirely reasonable. Think; before we received the noble Messenger's ﷺ guidance, what knowledge of Īmān did we possess? What constituted objective good action and prescribed worship in our own estimation? We had no idea. Allāh says:

[96] Al-Qur'ān 49:5
[97] *Jāmiʿ al-Bayān fī Ta'wīl al-Qur'ān* – Imām al-Ṭabarī
[98] *Tafsīr al-Taḥrīr wa al-Tanwīr* – Ibn ʿĀshūr

> وَكَذَٰلِكَ أَوْحَيْنَا إِلَيْكَ رُوحًا مِّنْ أَمْرِنَا ۚ مَا كُنتَ تَدْرِي مَا الْكِتَابُ وَلَا الْإِيمَانُ وَلَٰكِن جَعَلْنَاهُ نُورًا نَّهْدِي بِهِ مَن نَّشَاءُ مِنْ عِبَادِنَا ۚ وَإِنَّكَ لَتَهْدِي إِلَىٰ صِرَاطٍ مُّسْتَقِيمٍ
>
> *Accordingly, We have revealed to you a Rūḥ by Our command. You had no idea of what the Book was, nor faith. Nonetheless We have made it a Light by which We guide those of Our slaves We will. Truly you are guiding to a Straight Path.*[99]

The Messenger ﷺ taught us how to worship and introduced those same good actions that we now fear becoming null and void. How, then, can those actions be considered good if the director to those actions is undermined? Hence, his veneration is inevitably linked to the validity of our actions.[100] Disrespecting the Messenger ﷺ derides the idea that we have done Islāmically good actions, as contempt of the source entails contempt of what emerges from it, hence actions cannot stand.

In his Tafsīr, Muḥammad Metwalī al-Shaʿrāwī says:

'Without doubt, the Messenger ﷺ is intensely kind and compassionate, but this kindness should never be exploited, seen as a license to diminish his awe and presence or allow it to be taken for granted. Since you had not found the Messenger of Allāh ﷺ in the Masjid addressing his duties towards the community, you should have assumed that he was either with his family or in seclusion with his Lord and left him alone.'[101]

The Recurring Address to the Believers

How does it make you feel to hear *'**You** who have Īmān'* again and again? It is repeated five times in *al-Ḥujurāt* alone and up to 87 times in the glorious Qur'ān. The companion ʿAbdullāh b. Masʿūd (raḍiy Allāhu ʿanhu) is reported to have said:

> إذا سمعت الله يقول، يا أيها الذين آمنوا، فأرعها سمعك، فإنه خير تأمر به، أو شر ينهى عنه

[99] Al-Qur'ān 42:52
[100] *Tafsīr al-Ḥujurāt* – Muḥammad Metwalī al-Shaʿrāwī
[101] *Tafsīr al-Ḥujurāt* – Muḥammad Metwalī al-Shaʿrāwī

> *"If you hear Allāh saying 'you who have Īmān' then listen carefully, since it is either something good you are being commanded to do or an evil you are being told to stay away from."*[102]

Allāh's call using Īmān in the Caller as an identifier intensely attaches those being called to the Caller. We are His slaves and have innate Īmān in Him and, as such, the call is very much a personal one. It has the bearing of a command but the undertones of honour and love. If you were to say to someone, *"I know you to be a person of virtue, honesty, and trust, can you look after my belongings?"* What will their reaction be? Can anything besides honesty and trust be expected from an attentive addressee? When you hear, *'You who have Īmān'*, this is *you* being called, praised, and loved, and at the same time asked to live up to the expectation and commitment!

It further informs that the One advising is advising in truth, for He is the Truth. It shows that such advice is of real importance to Him and thus what follows cannot be received flippantly. It is a *crucial* warning or instruction. Likewise, with due diligence, concern, and self-evaluation, the addressee should ask *why* Allāh is reprimanding those who have raised their voices. Was it me? Was it something I did?

Effort Breeds Taqwā

Imām Aḥmad reports that a letter was written to ʿUmar (raḍiy Allāhu ʿanhu) that asked:

> *"Leader of the believers, what is better, a man who does not crave sin, nor acts upon it, or a man who craves sin, but does not act upon it?" ʿUmar replied, "Those who crave sin and do not act upon it." Then he quoted the verse of al-Ḥujurāt, "Those whose hearts Allāh has tested for Taqwā."*[103,104]

The analogy of metal ore mentioned in the Tafsīr applies squarely onto the heart. For the ore of one's heart to be melted away it must be subjected to the intensity or heat of desire. If withstood and resisted, that heart will accommodate *Taqwā* as per the verse. The word *'imtaḥana'* also sits on the template of a hyperbolised verb, implying that such a process is naturally severe and painful.

---

[102] *Al-Zuhd wa al-Raqā'iq* – Ibn al-Mubārak

[103] Al-Qur'ān 49:3

[104] Mentioned in *Tafsīr al-Qur'ān al-ʿAẓīm* – Ibn Kathīr. There is discontinuity in the chain of transmission as Mujāhid did not meet ʿUmar (*rady Allāhu 'anhu*), but the meaning of the narration holds true.

Who is not struggling with one desire or another unique to that person? Use the intensity of *your* tribulation as a yardstick to determine what Allāh will reward you for and which, if resisted, will likely purify your heart the most. Allāh has given you the opportunity to say *no* to those impulses and earn His pleasure. Perhaps through your determined avoidance, you end up reaching greater levels than those not struggling to begin with.

Consider the seven who will be shaded under the Throne of Allāh on a Day when there is no shade but His. Have you ever asked yourself what the *common action* was that grouped them in that same place and situation? They are:

> إِمَامٌ عَادِلٌ، وَشَابٌّ نَشَأَ فِي عِبَادَةِ اللَّهِ، وَرَجُلٌ ذَكَرَ اللَّهَ فِي خَلَاءٍ فَفَاضَتْ عَيْنَاهُ، وَرَجُلٌ قَلْبُهُ مُعَلَّقٌ فِي المَسْجِدِ، وَرَجُلَانِ تَحَابَّا فِي اللَّهِ، وَرَجُلٌ دَعَتْهُ امْرَأَةٌ ذَاتُ مَنْصِبٍ وَجَمَالٍ إِلَى نَفْسِهَا، قَالَ، إِنِّي أَخَافُ اللَّهَ، وَرَجُلٌ تَصَدَّقَ بِصَدَقَةٍ فَأَخْفَاهَا حَتَّى لَا تَعْلَمَ شِمَالُهُ مَا صَنَعَتْ يَمِينُهُ
>
> *"A just ruler; a youth who grew up with the worship of Allāh; a person whose heart is attached to the Masājid; two men who love and meet each other and depart from each other for the sake of Allāh; a man whom an extremely beautiful woman seduces him [for illicit relations] but he [rejects this offer and] says, 'I fear Allāh'; a man who gives in charity and conceals it [to such an extent] that the left hand does not know what the right has given; and a man who remembers Allāh in solitude and his eyes become tearful."*[105]

By the universal concept of reaping what you sow, there must be a common denominator between them. To answer this, Ibn Rajab al-Hanbali mentions:

> *"These seven, on the surface, did different things, but each meet under a single meaning. That is their struggle against their own selves and their defiance of their desires. This needs intense practice and restraint in the face of one's desires, irritations or greed. Enduring this inflicts severe hardship on oneself and immense pain. The* ***heart almost burns*** *from the fire of desires or anger when it billows, if not extinguished by performing those desires. Without doubt, the reward of being patient when the heat intensifies on that standing (the Day of Judgement), when there is no shadow in which people can shade themselves to protect themselves*

---

[105] *Ṣaḥīḥ* Bukhārī and Muslim on the authority of Abu Hurairah (raḍiy Allāhu ʿanhu)

> *from the sun's heat is that these seven will be in the shade of Allāh. They will not experience pain [from] that Day's heat as a reward for their patience when they [had] experienced the fire of desire or anger in the Dunya."*[106]

Good Physical Actions Can Purify the Spirit

Allāh mentions the purification of hearts alongside lowering the voice in the Messenger's ﷺ presence despite one being physical and the other being spiritual. Clearly, our physical behaviours, actions, and even appearance have an impact on our spiritual state. Speech will impact the heart, and 'spirituality' – or rather *Taqwā* – is not necessarily something one can easily perceive. Giving charity is not thought of as a typical 'spiritual' action but it nonetheless increases *Taqwā*, as does honouring the parents, walking to the masjid, performing Ḥajj, and so on. The way we behave with people around us in everyday life will also have an impact on our spiritual wellbeing. The opposite is also true.

After speaking about defrauding people financially – a physical transaction – Allāh informs us about the effect of such an action on people's own hearts:

> كَلَّا ۖ بَلْ ۜ رَانَ عَلَىٰ قُلُوبِهِم مَّا كَانُوا يَكْسِبُونَ
>
> *No! But that which they used to commit has covered their hearts with rust.*[107]

Just as raising one's voice in the Prophet's ﷺ presence can enter one into a cycle of spiritual regression, good action of all sorts increases Taqwā, and Taqwā increases good actions of all sorts until a person enters an upward cycle of doing better and better! And Allāh knows best. All praise and thanks are due to Him alone.

[106] See *Fatḥ al-Bāri* by Ibn Rajab al-Hanbalī – translated to this author's best effort. The Imām seemingly collects the seven categories under resistance to temptation (such as sexual desires) and resistance to anger (such as being a just ruler despite being able to punish opponents).
[107] Al-Qur'ān 83:14

THOSE WHO CALLED OUT THE MESSENGER

He taught us the meaning of good action; he is Allāh's chosen one on Earth, and His greatest Messenger, ﷺ. Ḥassan (raḍiy Allāhu ʿanhu) would say in his famous couplets:

> 'My eye has never seen anything more perfect than you. Women have never conceived more beautiful than you. You have been created free of any defect. It is as if you were created as you willed.'

Who raised their voices behind the Prophet's apartments, and how did the noble companions respond? Those who called the Prophet ﷺ were from a tribe by the name of Banī Tamīm. We know that they came to Madīnah in the ninth year of the Hijrah, also known as the 'Year of the Delegates' (*ʿĀm al-Wufūd*). The visiting group comprised of around 70 or more individuals. It is said that they came to Madīnah to ransom some of their captives who were taken by the companions after stopping some of their fellow tribesmen from paying the Zakāh duty to the Messenger of Allāh ﷺ.

The group was therefore one of varying degrees of devotion, and some of Banī Tamīm's clans had still not embraced Islām. They entered the Masjid in the middle of the afternoon, during what is called *al-Qā'ilah* which is a short period of rest. The Prophet ﷺ was resting in one of his wives' apartments.[108]

Shown overleaf is an *approximate* outline of *al-Masjid al-Nabawī* in the Prophetic era and the arrangement of the Prophet's ﷺ apartments.

[108] *Al-Jāmiʿ li Aḥkām al-Qur'ān* – Imām Qurṭubī

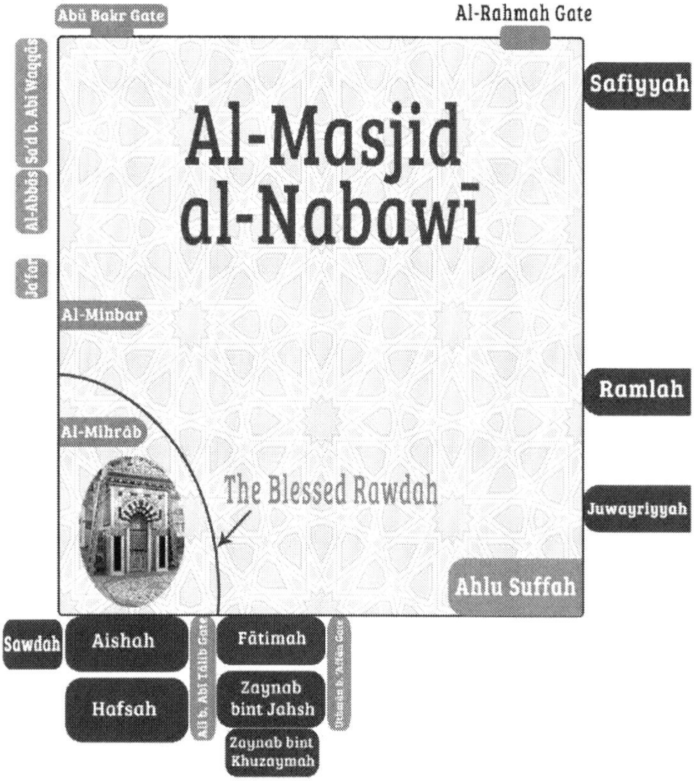

Notice how the majority of the Prophet's apartments are clustered next to the purified *Rawdah* (garden), which is a section of Paradise as per the ḥadīth of the Messenger ﷺ:

> مَا بَيْنَ بَيْتِي وَمِنْبَرِي رَوْضَةٌ مِنْ رِيَاضِ الْجَنَّةِ
>
> *"Between my house and my pulpit there is a garden of the gardens of Paradise."*[109]

Historical accounts mention that members of Banī Tamīm had positioned themselves near the Prophet's apartments. In a raised voice they demanded, *"Muḥammad! Bring out three of your men [to duel us] for we are worthy of being praised, and our offence is a disgrace."*[110] This type of provocation to a verbal duel was

[109] *Ṣaḥīḥ* Bukhārī and Muslim on the authority of Abu Hurairah (raḍiy Allāhu ʿanhu)
[110] *Tafsīr al-Qur'ān al-ʿAẓīm* – Ibn Kathīr and others

commonplace in Arabia at the time. The duel would involve the two parties mentioning each other's traits and achievements before determining the better of the two. They continued, *"We came to outdo you in status."*

Some narrations specify that the individual who called out was al-Aqraʿ b. Ḥābis who may have been their leader or representative. Since it is customary to attribute the actions of a leader to those who follow, the verse uses the plural construct, *'yunādūnak'* (*those who call out to you*). This is similar to attributing a crime to a group saying 'they' did it, even when only one person physically executes the crime. It is also possible that they *all* participated in calling out the noble Messenger ﷺ in one way or another.

According to other exegetes, the second verse was revealed concerning the two great Shaykhs, Abu Bakr and ʿUmar (raḍiy Allāhu ʿanhumā).[111] Contextually, this would have likely been after the event had elapsed and Banī Tamīm had embraced Islām. Now, needing to elect a leader over their locality, the two Sheikhs counselled the Messenger ﷺ as to who should be appointed. Ibn Abī Mulaikah said:

> كَادَ الخَيِّرانِ أَنْ يَهْلَكَا، أَبُو بَكْرٍ وَعُمَرُ، رَضِيَ اللَّهُ عَنْهُمَا
>
> *"The two select, righteous men were about to be ruined, Abu Bakr and ʿUmar (raḍiy Allāhu 'anhumā)."*[112]

He continued:

> رَفَعَا أَصْوَاتَهُمَا عِنْدَ النَّبِيِّ حِينَ قَدِمَ عَلَيْهِ رَكْبُ بَنِي تَمِيمٍ. فَأَشَارَ أَحَدُهُمَا بِالْأَقْرَعِ بْنِ حَابِسٍ أَخِي بَنِي مُجَاشِعٍ وَأَشَارَ الْآخَرُ بِرَجُلٍ آخَرَ – قَالَ نَافِعٌ، لَا أَحْفَظُ اسْمَهُ – فَقَالَ أَبُو بَكْرٍ لِعُمَرَ، مَا أَرَدْتَ إِلَّا خِلَافِي. قَالَ، مَا أَرَدْتُ خِلَافَكَ. فَارْتَفَعَتْ أَصْوَاتُهُمَا فِي ذَلِكَ فَأَنْزَلَ اللَّهُ، يَا أَيُّهَا الَّذِينَ آمَنُوا لَا تَرْفَعُوا أَصْوَاتَكُمْ فَوْقَ صَوْتِ النَّبِيِّ وَلَا تَجْهَرُوا لَهُ بِالْقَوْلِ كَجَهْرِ بَعْضِكُمْ لِبَعْضٍ الْآيَةَ. قَالَ ابْنُ الزُّبَيْرِ، فَمَا كَانَ عُمَرُ يسمعُ رَسُولَ اللَّهِ بَعْدَ هَذِهِ الْآيَةِ حَتَّى يَسْتَفْهِمَهُ
>
> *"They raised their voice in the presence of the Prophet ﷺ when the delegate of Banī Tamīm came to the Prophet ﷺ. One of them recommended that al-Aqraʿ b. Ḥābis al-Tamīmī al-Handhalī be appointed as their chief, while the other recommended*

---

[111] *Tafsīr al-Qur'ān al-ʿAẓīm* – Ibn Kathīr
[112] *Ṣaḥīḥ* Bukhārī on the authority of Ibn Abī Mulaikah

> *another. Abu Bakr said to 'Umar, 'You only intended to oppose me.' 'Umar said, 'I did not intend to oppose you!' Gradually, their voices grew louder in front of the Prophet ﷺ whereupon it was revealed, 'You who have Īmān! Do not raise your voices above the voice of the Prophet.'"*

Ibn al-Zubair said, *"From then on, when 'Umar talked to the Prophet, he would talk [so quietly] that the Prophet ﷺ would ask him to repeat what he said."* In another ḥadīth, Abu Bakr (raḍiy Allāhu 'anhu) said:

> لَمَّا نَزَلَتْ هَذِهِ الْآيَةُ، يَا أَيُّهَا الَّذِينَ آمَنُوا لَا تَرْفَعُوا أَصْوَاتَكُمْ فَوْقَ صَوْتِ النَّبِيِّ، قُلْتُ، يَا رَسُولَ اللهِ، وَاللهِ لَا أُكَلِّمُكَ إلا كأخي السّرار
>
> *"When the verse 'You who have Īmān! Do not raise your voices above the voice of the Prophet' was revealed, I said 'Messenger of Allāh, by Allāh I will not speak to you except as one telling a secret to another.'"*[113]

Allāh then revealed the third verse (*'those who lower their voices'*) as an interjectory statement. It addresses the natural curiosity of those who hear the admonition will have regarding the opposite group – those who lower their voices in the presence of the Messenger of Allāh. It also comes to promptly allay the fears of those who may have thought they were the intended in the first address.[114]

Qur'anic exegetes agree that this distinct reward and praise is primarily directed at Abu Bakr and 'Umar (raḍiy Allāhu 'anhu) because they both never spoke to the Messenger of Allāh ﷺ after that except by whispering,[115] rushing to apply the directive. By extension, this directive applies to each and every individual who lowers their voice in the Prophet's revered physical presence or figuratively under his *Sunnah*.

The Companions Ready for Any Occasion

When Banī Tamīm sought to have a duel both in sermon (*Khitābah*) and poetry (*Shi'r*), the companions of the Messenger of Allāh ﷺ were well-prepared and ready to meet like for like. Collectively, they mastered every art and skill necessary for the

[113] Al-Hākim on the authority of Abu Hurairah (raḍiy Allāhu 'anhu)

[114] *Tafsīr al-Taḥrīr wa al-Tanwīr* – Ibn 'Āshūr

[115] *Tafsīr al-Taḥrīr wa al-Tanwīr* – Ibn 'Āshūr

function of society, and they directed each of these to the service of Allāh and His Messenger ﷺ, ready for any challenge. Al-Aqraʿ stepped forth with a challenge to the Messenger ﷺ of poetic expression:

أَتَيْناكَ كَيْما يَعْرِفُ النّاسُ فَضْلَنا إذا خالَفُونا عِنْدَ ذِكْرِ المكارِمِ
وأنّا رُؤُوسُ النّاسِ مِن كُلِّ مَعْشَرٍ وأنْ لَيْسَ في أرْضِ الحِجازِ كَدارِمِ
وأنَّ لنا المِرْباعَ في كُلِّ غارَةٍ تَكُونُ بِنَجْدٍ أوْ بِأرْضِ التَّهائِمِ

"We came to you and people are well aware of our nobility, particularly if we are opposed when nobility is mentioned. We are leaders, and in all of Ḥijāz there are none like Dārim.[116] And to us belong the spoils in every assault in the land of Najd or Tihāmah."[117]

The Prophet ﷺ was eager to address their contest with what is better. He said, turning to his formidable poet Ḥassān b. Thābit (raḍiy Allāhu ʿanhu), *"Stand up and reply to him."* Ḥassān stood and determinedly recited:

بَنِي دارِمٍ لا تَفْخَرُونَ إنَّ فَخْرَكم يَصِيرُ وبالًا عِنْدَ ذِكْرِ المكارِمِ
هَبُلْتُمْ عَلَيْنا تَفْخَرُونَ وأنْتُمْ لَنا خَوَّلٌ مِن بَيْنِ ظِئْرٍ وخادِمِ
فَإنْ كُنْتُمْ جِئْتُمْ لِحَقْنِ دِمائِكم وأمْوالِكم أنْ يُقَسَّمُوا في المقاسِمِ
فَلا تَجْعَلُوا لِلَّهِ نِدًّا وأسْلِمُوا ولا تَفْخَرُوا عِنْدَ النَّبِيِّ بِدارِمِ
وإلّا ورَبِّ البَيْتِ قَدْ مالَتِ القَنا عَلى هامِكم بِالمرْهِفاتِ الصَّوارِمِ

"Banī Dārim, do not boast, for it is a curse when [true] nobilities are mentioned. You have boasted despite being our pitied servants. If you have come seeking to protect your blood and wealth from distribution, then embrace Islām and stop bragging about 'Dārim' in the presence of the Messenger. Otherwise, by the Lord of the House, our spears and swords will be directed at your feeble heads and bodies."

Al-Aqraʿ b. Ḥābis stood taken aback and said, *"What is this? Our spokesperson spoke, but yours was better than ours. And our poet spoke but your poet was better than ours."* Then he approached the Messenger ﷺ and declared, *"I testify there is no*

[116] *Dārim* – a sub-tribe of Banī Tamīm
[117] *Tihāmah* could be a reference to Makkah. See *Lisān al-ʿArab*

Lord worthy of worship but Allāh, and that you are the Messenger of Allāh." The Messenger ﷺ replied, *"Nothing you did before this will harm you."*[118]

Notice how the Prophetic community was neither passive in the face of denigration, nor unprepared. Here, the noble Messenger ﷺ ensured that he utilised the same, impactful modes and arts of communication known to the Arabs. The underlying message is that if you insist on poetry, we have more sublime poetry and are prepared to fight the battle *you* choose. In fact, the Prophet used to say to Ḥassan (raḍiy Allāhu ʿanhu):

> *"Satirise [with poetry] against the Quraish, for it is more grievous to them than the hurt of an arrow." Ḥassan replied, "You have called for this lion who strikes [the enemies] with his tail." He then brought out his tongue and began to move it and said, "By Him Who has sent you with Truth, I shall tear them with my tongue as leather is torn."*

ʿĀ'ishah (raḍiy Allāhu ʿanha), the narrator, said, "I heard Allāh's Messenger ﷺ saying to Ḥassan:

> إِنَّ رُوحَ الْقُدُسِ لاَ يَزَالُ يُؤَيِّدُكَ مَا نَافَحْتَ عَنِ اللَّهِ وَرَسُولِهِ
>
> *"Verily Rūḥ al-Qudus [Jibrīl (ʿalayhi al-Salām)] will continue to help you so long as you put up a defence on behalf of Allāh and His Messenger."*[119]

From then on, Ḥassān (raḍiy Allāhu ʿanhu) worked alongside Abu Bakr (raḍiy Allāhu ʿanhu) who was a master of Arabian genealogy. He would 'spice up' his poetry with Abu Bakr's immersed knowledge of some of the family controversies, infamies, and mortifying nuances that the Prophet's detractors prayed would stay hidden. He would say:

ألا أبلغْ أبا سفيانَ عني　　　فأنتَ مجوفٌ نخبٌ هواءُ

وأن سيوفنا تركتك عبدا　　　وعبد الدار سادتها الإماء

"Tell Abu Sufyan about me. Because you (Abu Sufyān) are in fact a
hollow, gaseous coward. Our swords have left you a slave.
As for ʿAbdu al-Dār, its leaders are in fact its bondwomen...

[118] *Rūḥ al-Maʿāny* – al-Alusi, who references Ibn Hishām's *Sīrah*
[119] *Ṣaḥīḥ* Muslim on the authority of ʿĀ'ishah (raḍiy Allāhu ʿanha)

هجوتَ محمداً، فأجبتُ عنهُ   وعندَ اللهِ في ذاكَ الجزاءُ

أَتَهْجُوهُ، وَلَسْتَ لَهُ بِكُفْءٍ   فَشَرُّكُما لِخَيْرِكُمَا الفِداءُ

"You satirised against Muḥammad, but I answered on his behalf. And with Allāh, for this will be the reward. Do you satirise against him whilst you are not his equal? [After all], the worst of us are bound to ransom our best."[120]

The Prophetic community was equipped to address the particular *challenges of the time* without shying away from using the *medium of the time*. Their areas of service varied; some were orators, others poets, warriors, scholars or medics. Others still were tillers, homemakers or wealthy businessmen, and they all operated as *one unit* and served *one cause*. Had they not seen their own skills as indispensable, and stepped up to the mark in their unique areas of delivery, the Prophetic community would have been left weak and exposed.

If every individual was identical in skill and area of expertise, they could not have bred a firm, complementary communal structure. Such is a pertinent lesson for us in the modern day. Eradicating exceptionally crucial roles, such as those naturally attuned to the Muslim wife and mother, for instance, exposes the family, which is the core of the community, to all types of problems and corruptions. Though it is great to be ambitious, we need not deform our own skills or forgo our own areas of responsibility simply to replicate others, as we are each valuable pieces in a large, symbiotic communal structure.

Finally, Banu Tamīm's encounter with the companions demonstrates that the latter did not suffer an inferiority complex. They were active in parading the excellence of their values and ways and firmly countered defamation, not least when it came from valueless individuals. Today, we are in dire need of Ḥassāns to likewise use current day effective media channels to satirise and expose the mortifications, corruptions, and controversies of media moguls, Islāmophobic pawns, and populists, and Allāh is the source of strength.

The Personal Impact of the Qur'ān on the Companions

Prior to Ḥassān's (raḍiy Allāhu ʿanhu) presentation, the orator (*Khatīb*) who challenged Banī Tamīm and defended the Messenger ﷺ and the Muslims was a companion by the name of Thābit b. Qais (raḍiy Allāhu ʿanhu). He was elected *Khatīb*

[120] This latter verse of poetry is known as the 'most equitable poetic verse an Arab has ever said' for its power and perfect revenge for the sake of the Messenger of Allāh ﷺ.

of the Anṣār because of his sound articulation and loud voice and, as such, would often be the Prophet's spokesman when receiving delegations. Anas b. Mālik (raḍiy Allāhu ʿanhu) narrates that when the verse of *al-Ḥujurāt, 'Do not raise your voices above the voice of the Prophet'* was revealed, Thābit confined himself to his house and said, *"I am from the people of Hell."* Thābit's absence was felt and the Messenger of Allāh ﷺ turned to Saʿd b. Muʿādh (or Ibn ʿUbādah)[121] asking, *"Abu 'Amr, how is Thābit? Has he fallen sick?"* Saʿd replied, *"He is my neighbour and I have not heard of him falling sick."*

When Saʿd checked up on Thābit, Thābit said, *"This verse [of al-Ḥujurāt] was revealed, and you are well aware that amongst all of you, my voice is louder than that of the Messenger of Allāh, and so I am from the people of Hell."* Saʿd informed the Messenger of Allāh ﷺ who replied, *"No, rather he is one of the people of Paradise."* Anas, the narrator comments:

"We used to see him (Thābit) walking between us whilst knowing that he is going to Paradise." Then on the day of Yamāmah, during the battle against Musailamah the Liar (*al-Kadhdhāb*), Thābit emerged wearing his death shroud, rebuking the soldiers who had retreated. He fought relentlessly until he fell as a martyr and the prophecy was fulfilled.[122] May Allāh be pleased with Thābit.

If the companion who dedicated his voice in the service of Allāh and His Messenger ﷺ felt that this verse addressed him, how much *more* does it address those who talk over ḥadīths, interrupt verses being recited or quoted, or throw evidences at one another in arguments? How does it affect our demeanour and respect we show the scholars of Islām, the 'inheritors of Prophets' as our Messenger ﷺ informed us? The companions not only applied the fullest extent of Allāh's words, but often went to excesses in their erring on the side of caution if they felt it was remotely possible that a verse admonished them.

Allāh Admonishes the Best

With this we learn that the elite of the ummah are not free from admonition. In fact, in certain Qur'ānic instances, even the Prophet ﷺ was mildly reproved by Allāh and, being His Messenger, none save Allāh can reprove him. As representatives of the Messenger ﷺ, Islām's leaders are also in need of admonition if they fall short. Naturally, the type and sternness of the admonition is closely associated with what the admonisher would have otherwise *expected* of the subject. A leader is held to a much higher standard than a layman. Recall the discussion on reasons for revelation above. Compare the threat of actions being rendered null to the two Sheikhs of the

---

[121] It was most likely Ibn ʿUbādah (raḍiy Allāhu ʿanhu) as Saʿd (raḍiy Allāhu ʿanhu) had been martyred long before this event

[122] *Ṣaḥīḥ* Muslim on the authority of Anas b. Mālik (raḍiy Allāhu ʿanhu)

ummah with the less stern address to Islām's new entrants. In the latter admonition we read:

> *As for those who call out to you from outside your private quarters, most of them do not use their intellect.*[123]

How intriguing that Abu Bakr and ʿUmar (raḍiy Allāhu ʿanhumā) received the sterner admonition for debating in the Messenger's presence when their misconduct pales in comparison to those who shouted threats to outdo the Messenger! But Abu Bakr and ʿUmar (raḍiy Allāhu ʿanhumā) are by no means your ordinary Muslims. As the front-runners of humanity, the style of their reproach corresponds. Importantly, this reproach did not negatively affect their Īmān, but instead, perfected it. The same sternness with Islām's new entrants, whose Īmān had not taken a firm hold, could have been disconcerting and may have had the opposite effect; hence the almost excusatory statement Allāh delivers them.

Remember these techniques when addressing Muslims who are at different levels of devotion. And Allāh knows best.

[123] Al-Qur'ān 49:4

SECTION 2: VERIFYING NEWS AND OBEYING RIGHTEOUS LEADERSHIP

A*l-Ḥujurāt*'s first section of five verses outlined the manners with Allāh and His Messenger, and the specific and exclusive behaviour a Muslim must exhibit towards the Final Messenger ﷺ, who was sent to complete the divine message and perfect the best manners. We recognised that no opinion or action should precede his. No voice should outdo his, neither in his presence, in the vicinity of his purified grave, over his reported directives or general Sunnah, nor in the sittings of his inheritors who are the scholars of Islām.

As a mercy to mankind, the Messenger ﷺ built a community upon the finest ethics. Putting Allāh and His Prophet first appropriately structures the ummah, such that it is protected first from vice, then conflict, and a subsequent disunity. Whoever overlooks Allāh and the Prophet's prerogative of being *first* is none but a deviator, rebellious one or '*Fāsiq*'.

It naturally follows that giving precedence to that *Fāsiq* brings about vice, conflict and disunity. Such conflict impacts the followers of the Messenger ﷺ and, as a result, the Messenger ﷺ himself for '*your suffering is distressing to him.*'[124] In this way, this second section of *al-Ḥujurāt* too is about not harming the Prophet of Allāh ﷺ in any way.[125]

---

[124] Al-Qur'ān 9:128

[125] *Naẓm al-Durar fī Tanāsub al-Āyāt wa al-Suwar* – al-Biqa'ī

Verses 6-8

> يا أَيُّهَا الَّذينَ آمَنوا إِن جاءَكُم فاسِقٌ بِنَبَإٍ فَتَبَيَّنوا أَن تُصيبوا قَومًا بِجَهالَةٍ فَتُصبِحوا عَلىٰ ما فَعَلتُم نادِمينَ ۝ وَاعلَموا أَنَّ فيكُم رَسولَ اللَّهِ ۚ لَو يُطيعُكُم في كَثيرٍ مِنَ الأَمرِ لَعَنِتُّم وَلٰكِنَّ اللَّهَ حَبَّبَ إِلَيكُمُ الإيمانَ وَزَيَّنَهُ في قُلوبِكُم وَكَرَّهَ إِلَيكُمُ الكُفرَ وَالفُسوقَ وَالعِصيانَ ۚ أُولٰئِكَ هُمُ الرّاشِدونَ ۝ فَضلًا مِنَ اللَّهِ وَنِعمَةً ۚ وَاللَّهُ عَليمٌ حَكيمٌ
>
> *You who have Īmān! if a deviator brings you a report, scrutinise it carefully in case you attack people in ignorance and so come to greatly regret what you have done. Know that the Messenger of Allāh is among you. If he were to obey you in many things, you would suffer for it. However, Allāh has given you love of Īmān and made it pleasing to your hearts, and has made Kufr, deviance and disobedience hateful to you. People such as these are rightly guided. It is a great favour from Allāh and a blessing. Allāh is All-Knowing, All-Wise.*[126]

Verse 6

Once again addressing the people of Īmān, Allāh says:

> يا أَيُّهَا الَّذينَ آمَنوا إِن جاءَكُم فاسِقٌ بِنَبَإٍ فَتَبَيَّنوا أَن تُصيبوا قَومًا بِجَهالَةٍ فَتُصبِحوا عَلىٰ ما فَعَلتُم نادِمينَ
>
> *You who have Īmān! If a deviator brings you a report, scrutinise it carefully in case you attack people in ignorance and so come to greatly regret what you have done.*[127]

Imām al-Ṭabarī writes on these verses:

---

[126] Al-Qur'ān 49:6-8
[127] Al-Qur'ān 49:6

'You who have believed in the truthfulness of Allāh and His Messenger, if a deviator brings you a report about a group of people then scrutinise it.'

Other authentic Qur'ānic recitations (*Qirā'āt*) mention *'fatathabbatū'* rather than *'fatabayyanū'*. In both cases, the meaning is to wait until you can establish the veracity of the report and not rush to accept it. It can be said that, more specifically, *'tathabut'* is to establish the veracity of the report itself, while *'tabayyun'* is to go further and establish the circumstances surrounding the report.[128]

'Take the time to establish its veracity just in case you end up inflicting anything on an innocent people out of ignorance, and by doing so regret both your unfounded accusation and the action you took as a result.'[129]

While Muḥammad Metwalī al-Sha'rāwī comments:

'The categorical mention of regret is because this is what is anticipated of a Mu'min after having mistakenly fallen into sin. And regretting a sin is the very first step of repentance.'[130]

This is the third call. In it we are introduced to the mannerisms Muslims should exhibit towards one another. It is not preceded with a conjunction (*ḥarf 'atf*) like 'and' which would say *'**and** you who have Īmān!'*; rather, it starts afresh with *'You who have Īmān!'* This gives the statement and what follows it individual emphasis and importance, as it is a new and individually-titled section of injunctions. A *'Fāsiq'* is a person who has *'Fusūq'*, which is to do what Islām ranks as a major sin (*kabā'ir*). Some have said that *Fāsiq* in this instance means a liar (*Kādhib*).[131] We will shed more light on this later.

The use of the conditional device 'if' (*in*), instead of 'when' (*idhā*), implies that such a circumstance should be rare or exceptional and by no means the norm. *'In case you attack people in ignorance'* then lays out the consequence of inventing news and should be read as a warning to those planning to do so. *'[T]o greatly regret what you have done'* implies, from a religious perspective, that the sin of attacking or blaming others on the basis of false news is not only on the originator of that news but on those who act upon it.[132]

---

[128] *'Umar al-Muqbil – Qawā'id Qur'āniyyāh.* For instance, it may be true that a man was walking with a woman in the middle of the night (*'tathabut'*), but did you establish who the woman was (*'tabayyun'*)?

[129] *Jāmi' al-Bayān fī Ta'wīl al-Qur'ān* – Imām al-Ṭabarī

[130] *Tafsīr al-Ḥujurāt* – Muḥammad Metwalī al-Sha'rāwī

[131] *Tafsīr al-Taḥrīr wa al-Tanwīr* – Ibn 'Āshūr

[132] *Tafsīr al-Taḥrīr wa al-Tanwīr* – Ibn 'Āshūr

The Emphasis of Repetition

We explored how repeating *'you who have Īmān'* causes an individual to feel curiosity and anticipation, and thus attention to what is essential. Repetition of address throughout the Qur'ān has the same effect. In *Sūrat Luqmān*, the wise man's discourse of advice to his son demonstrates this. Focus on his advice preceded by *'my son'* against those merely connected by the conjunction 'and':

> يَا بُنَيَّ لَا تُشْرِكْ بِاللَّهِ إِنَّ الشِّرْكَ لَظُلْمٌ عَظِيمٌ ... يَا بُنَيَّ إِنَّهَا إِن تَكُ مِثْقَالَ حَبَّةٍ مِّنْ خَرْدَلٍ فَتَكُن فِي صَخْرَةٍ أَوْ فِي السَّمَاوَاتِ أَوْ فِي الْأَرْضِ يَأْتِ بِهَا اللَّهُ إِنَّ اللَّهَ لَطِيفٌ خَبِيرٌ ۞ يَا بُنَيَّ أَقِمِ الصَّلَاةَ...
>
> *"**My son,** do not **associate anything with Allāh**. Associating others with Him is a terrible wrong...*[133] ***My son,** even if something weighs as little as a mustard-seed and is inside a rock or anywhere else in the Heavens or Earth, Allāh will bring it out...*[134] ***My son, establish Ṣalāh...**"*[135]

In the next verse he says:

> وَلَا تُصَعِّرْ خَدَّكَ لِلنَّاسِ وَلَا تَمْشِ فِي الْأَرْضِ مَرَحًا إِنَّ اللَّهَ لَا يُحِبُّ كُلَّ مُخْتَالٍ فَخُورٍ
>
> *"**And** do not avert your face from people out of haughtiness **and** do not strut about arrogantly on the Earth. Allāh does not love anyone who is vain or boastful."*[136]

Each time the matter is related to Islām's fundamental creed (*'Aqīdah*), a greatness such as Allāh's Oneness (*Tawḥīd*) or establishing Ṣalāh, he repeats his address *'yā bunay'*. But for those matters related to interacting with Allāh's creatures, he uses the conjunction 'and'.[137]

---

133 Al-Qur'ān 31:13
134 Al-Qur'ān 31:16
135 Al-Qur'ān 31:17
136 Al-Qur'ān 31:18
137 *Tafsīr al-Ḥujurāt* – Muḥammad Metwalī al-Sha'rāwī

Who is a Fāsiq?

Who is a *Fāsiq*? Some have said that a *Fāsiq* is a person who indulges in major sins or insists on lesser sins to such a degree that they totally outweigh his good deeds. In Islām, major sins are generally considered those with an associated penal punishment in the Qur'ān or authentic Sunnah. This, unsurprisingly, includes adultery, fornication, alcoholism, theft, unsubstantiated or uncorroborated accusations of fornication, and the like. Lesser sins encompass most other sins we accumulate in our daily lives. *Fāsiq* is not an easy accusation to throw around at those who commit lesser mistakes as a *Fāsiq* is usually easily identified from his or her outward insistence on unambiguous abominations.

Linguistically, the Arabs say, *'fasaqat al-rutabah'* when the inner pulp of a date separates (*fasaqat*) from its skin. When this happens, the pulp loses its surrounding protection, is exposed to pests and starts to decay. In much the same way, a Muslim is surrounded by the shield of *Īmān*. When a person slips out of this fortification, one becomes exposed to sin and, if acclimatised to it, becomes a *Fāsiq*. This person then becomes even more vulnerable to all types of pests, corrupters and further decay.[138]

Both the words *Fāsiq* and *Naba'* (news) are in the indefinite form. In other words, *Fāsiq* is not *al-Fāsiq*, and *Naba'* is not *al-Naba'*. Neither is particularised. This delivers the meaning that if ***any*** *Fāsiq* that can be described by that title, due to them being known for ***any*** type of *Fusūq* (noun – an action of deviance), brings ***any*** piece of news, scrutinise it. The type of *Fusūq* does not need to be of a particular sort, or specifically related to their trustworthiness. If a person's *Fusūq* is related to their open promiscuity or insistence on financial wrongdoing, for instance, that person falls under this category and their trustworthiness should be scrutinised.[139] This is because acclimatisation to *Fusūq* of *any* sort usually indicates that one's inner religious compass is fragile. The fact the *Fāsiq* could not protect themselves from harm, it stands to reason that they would be less willing, and likely unable, to protect society at large.

Who and How Do We Scrutinise?

How should the verse of scrutinising reports affect how we receive accounts in general? According to Ibn ʿĀshūr, a number of legal principles can be derived from the verse. Firstly, one must investigate the trustworthiness of the unknown person before accepting their witness or account. One is not presuming they are *Fāsiq*, but that their trustworthiness is yet to be determined. Thus, it is to prevent taking action against others on the basis of unverified news. Secondly, if a person cannot be known in any way, their statements should not be accepted. Thirdly, it is sufficient for a single

[138] *Tafsīr of al-Ḥujurāt* by Sheikh Muḥammad al-Shaʿrāwī

[139] *Tafsīr al-Taḥrīr wa al-Tanwīr* – Ibn ʿĀshūr

trustworthy person to come with a report or statement, or to provide a witness account for it to be accepted, except in cases where Islām explicitly demands more than one witness. Finally, the 'regret' mentioned in the verse indicates that if a person fails to adequately scrutinise and proceeds to take inappropriate action, he or she is also blameworthy.[140]

Thus, included in the address are: (i) the Prophet ﷺ; (ii) the scholars of Islām – in order to establish the principle of transferring knowledge and authority and when issuing legal verdicts; (iii) the leadership – so as to only rely on trustworthy accounts, and (iv) every individual who hears this verse until the end of time. And Allāh knows best.

---

[140] *Tafsīr al-Taḥrīr wa al-Tanwīr* – Ibn ʿĀshūr

HE CAME TO ELIMINATE YOUR SUFFERING

After calling believers to show due respect to the greatest Messenger and Seal of the Prophets ﷺ, Allāh cautioned that following he whose moral compass is fragile – the *Fāsiq* – is bound to bring regret. Regret not only for erring against an innocent people, but for carrying the religious burden of that crime. Every sin comes with its exhausting physical and spiritual burden, in this world and the next, that the Prophet ﷺ came to eliminate.

Verse 7

> وَاعلَموا أَنَّ فيكُم رَسولَ اللَّهِ ۚ لَو يُطيعُكُم في كَثيرٍ مِنَ الأَمرِ لَعَنِتُّم وَلٰكِنَّ اللَّهَ حَبَّبَ إِلَيكُمُ الإيمانَ
> وَزَيَّنَهُ في قُلوبِكُم وَكَرَّهَ إِلَيكُمُ الكُفرَ وَالفُسوقَ وَالعِصيانَ ۚ أُولٰئِكَ هُمُ الرّاشِدونَ
>
> *Know that the Messenger of Allāh is among you. If he were to obey you in many things, you would suffer for it. However, Allāh has given you love of Īmān and made it pleasing to your hearts, and has made Kufr, deviance, and disobedience hateful to you. People such as these are rightly guided.*[141]

'Know well, people of Īmān, that the Messenger of Allāh ﷺ is among you. As such, have Taqwā of Allāh, in case you say what is false or invent lies because Allāh conveys your news to him and guides him to what is right in his matters. Were the Messenger of Allāh to act upon your opinions, you would suffer difficulties and be fatigued in a lot of your affairs. Allāh has, however, given you the love of Īmān in Allāh and His Messenger.

You obey the Messenger of Allāh and are underneath his charge, and by this Allāh has saved you from that suffering. Moreover, Īmān has been perfected in your hearts, so you believed. Allāh has also made the denial of Allāh and disbelief in Him (Kufr), dishonesty[142] *(Fusūq), and doing what Allāh has prohibited by going against His Messenger and absconding from his instructions ('Isyān) disliked to you. These people are the followers of the path of truth (Rāshidūn).'*[143]

---

[141] Al-Qur'ān 49:7

[142] As is chosen in this instance by Imām al-Ṭabarī

[143] *Jāmi' al-Bayān fī Ta'wīl al-Qur'ān* – Imām al-Ṭabarī

Fusūq, as alluded to earlier, can refer to major sins, whilst *ʿIṣyān* can be a reference to lesser sins. With this understanding, the seventh verse outlines, in decreasing order of severity, three detestable things to the *Mu'min* who truly wishes to serve their own interest and is on a sound disposition: disbelief, major sins, and lesser sins.[144] Following this Qur'ānic style and content, one can wholesomely implore Allāh in the prophetic *Duʿā'*:

> اللَّهُمَّ حَبِّبْ إِلَيْنَا الْإِيمَانَ وَزَيِّنْهُ فِي قُلُوبِنَا، وَكَرِّهْ إِلَيْنَا الْكُفْرَ وَالْفُسُوقَ وَالْعِصْيَانَ وَاجْعَلْنَا مِنَ الرَّاشِدِينَ
>
> *"Allāh, make Īmān beloved to us and make it pleasing to our hearts, and make Kufr, deviance and disobedience hateful to us and make us of the rightly guided (Rāshidīn)."*[145]

The Messenger of Allāh ﷺ was among us. He, by transmission from the Creator, knew better our own interests, and was tempered by His Lord to be more concerned about us than our own selves. His opinions on our behalf are thus more beneficial to us than those we make for ourselves.[146]

Elsewhere, Allāh says:

> النَّبِيُّ أَوْلَىٰ بِالْمُؤْمِنِينَ مِنْ أَنفُسِهِمْ
>
> *The Prophet is more worthy of the Mu'minīn than themselves.*[147]

He is the worthiest of our obedience and loyalty and simultaneously more concerned for us than we are for one another.

Returning to this seventh verse of *Sūrah al-Ḥujurāt*, the placement of *'know that'* (*iʿlamū*) at the beginning creates a sense of anticipation and lends weight to what will follow, *'The Messenger of Allāh is among you'*. The companions already know that the Messenger ﷺ is among them, but the prompt warns them to be careful and heedful, as the Noble Messenger ﷺ is present and the heavenly link to Allāh through live revelation is still intact. Even after his physical presence, his guidance is ever-present in his Sunnah and legislation,[148] which are far superior to our own whims and desires.

---

[144] *Taysīr al-Karīm al-Raḥmān fī Tafsīr Kalām al-Mannān* – ʿAbdur-Raḥmān Al-Saʿdī
[145] Al-Haythamī, al-Bazzār and others on the authority of Rifāʿah b. Rāfiʿ (raḍiy Allāhu ʿanhu)
[146] *Tafsīr al-Qur'ān al-ʿAẓīm* – Ibn Kathīr
[147] Al-Qur'ān 33:6
[148] *Tafsīr al-Taḥrīr wa al-Tanwīr* – Ibn ʿĀshūr

The literal and linguistic construct of, *'know that the Messenger of Allāh is among you'* is in fact, *'know that **among you** is the Messenger of Allāh.'* This subtlety expresses that the Messenger of Allāh ﷺ is the main constituent. He is the essence, whilst you are his surrounding envelope. The value of an 'envelope' is determined by what it contains, not by its envelope. The construct furthermore accentuates that the *best* you can internalise within yourselves as humans is the Messenger of Allāh ﷺ and his guidance. The more of him you internalise, the more valuable you become and if it were not for him, nothing would have given you recognition or inner value.[149]

*'If he were to obey you in **many things**,'* were your wishes contrary to his, *'you would suffer for it.'* At the same time, 'many things' suggests there are many other areas that Islām gives Muslims the privilege to make their own judgements on. The Prophet ﷺ himself consulted the companions when he received no definitive divine inspiration, such as where to position the army on the day of Badr and what to do with the captives. *'However, Allāh has given you love of Īmān,'* includes the love of Islām itself, not only its inner convictions or belief system. Thus, Allāh has given you the love of Islām, Īmān, and the rules and regulations in the religion of Allāh brought by His Messenger ﷺ. Allāh says to His Prophet in another verse:

> فَلَا وَرَبِّكَ لَا يُؤْمِنُونَ حَتَّىٰ يُحَكِّمُوكَ فِيمَا شَجَرَ بَيْنَهُمْ ثُمَّ لَا يَجِدُوا فِي أَنفُسِهِمْ حَرَجًا مِّمَّا قَضَيْتَ وَيُسَلِّمُوا تَسْلِيمًا
>
> *No, by your Lord, they will not have Īmān until they make you their judge in the disputes that break out between them, and then find no resistance within themselves to what you decide and submit themselves completely.*[150]

Notice that *'**Allāh** has given you the love of Īmān'* and none, besides Him, granted *you* that love. Attributing this gift to the Almighty, using the greatest of Allāh's names – 'Allāh' – is to inspire effort and perseverance in *you*, the receiver. Consequently, you will struggle against any sinful inclination for the sake of Allāh by recalling that He gave you the love of Īmān to begin with.[151]

'You Would Suffer for It'

It may seem counter-intuitive that sinful desires bring about suffering. Surely it is more cumbersome to do what you are told. In the European era dubbed the

---

[149] *Tafsīr al-Ḥujurāt* by Sheikh Muḥammad Metwalī al-Sha'rāwī
[150] Al-Qur'ān 4:65
[151] *Tafsīr al-Ḥujurāt* by Sheikh Muḥammad Metwalī al-Sha'rāwī

'Enlightenment', people were told that godlessness, secularism and later versions of liberalism (read: doing whatever one desired) would be their salvation from dogmatic theocracies and make them *happy*. It takes little to prove how cock-eyed these philosophies were in seeking to address suffering in the 'free world', now beleaguered with depression and suicide.[152] It seems absurd to many that divine regulation can address human suffering and *liberate* them from the distressful fetters brought about by vice. This is, however, obvious to the Mu'min who recognises that the One Who Created knows what best serves the interests of His creatures:

> *...If he were to obey you in many things, you would suffer for it.*[153]

Allāh created us for Paradise, which is also our place of origin. We were removed from that home of comfort and happiness to another of fatigue and misery through the perception of unrestricted liberty. Iblīs, the *Shayṭān*, lost the company of Angels in the Heavens and became debased and rejected through the same. When the Pharaoh took liberty to claim divinity, boasting:

> وَنَادَىٰ فِرْعَوْنُ فِي قَوْمِهِ قَالَ يَا قَوْمِ أَلَيْسَ لِي مُلْكُ مِصْرَ وَهَٰذِهِ الْأَنْهَارُ تَجْرِي مِن تَحْتِيٓ أَفَلَا تُبْصِرُونَ
>
> *"Does not the kingdom of Egypt belong to me, and these rivers flowing beneath me; do you not see?"*[154]

The same water submerged him, bringing an end to much comfort and ease:

> كَمْ تَرَكُوا مِن جَنَّاتٍ وَعُيُونٍ ◊ وَزُرُوعٍ وَمَقَامٍ كَرِيمٍ ◊ وَنَعْمَةٍ كَانُوا فِيهَا فَاكِهِينَ ◊ كَذَٰلِكَ
> وَأَوْرَثْنَاهَا قَوْمًا آخَرِينَ

[152] According to NHS figures, ***one in four** females* in the UK and ***one in five** males* are clinically depressed. In the UK alone, up to *65 million* prescriptions for antidepressants were issued in 2016, *up by 100%* in 10 years. Suicide rates are staggeringly the highest amongst middle-aged and even middle-class men.
[153] Al-Qur'ān 49:7
[154] Al-Qur'ān 43:51

> *How many gardens and fountains they left behind, and ripe crops and noble residences. What* ***comfort*** *and* ***ease*** *they had delighted in! So it was. Yet We inherited these things to another people.*[155]

The devastating consequences of sinning against Allāh are so far-reaching that they enter into every part of a person's livelihood and every phase of a person's worldly existence and Hereafter. The Prophet ﷺ said:

> لَمْ تَظْهَرِ الْفَاحِشَةُ فِي قَوْمٍ قَطُّ حَتَّى يُعْلِنُوا بِهَا إِلاَّ فَشَا فِيهِمُ الطَّاعُونُ وَالأَوْجَاعُ الَّتِي لَمْ تَكُنْ مَضَتْ فِي أَسْلاَفِهِمُ الَّذِينَ مَضَوْا. وَلَمْ يَنْقُصُوا الْمِكْيَالَ وَالْمِيزَانَ إِلاَّ أُخِذُوا بِالسِّنِينَ وَشِدَّةِ الْمَؤُنَةِ وَجَوْرِ السُّلْطَانِ عَلَيْهِمْ. وَلَمْ يَمْنَعُوا زَكَاةَ أَمْوَالِهِمْ إِلاَّ مُنِعُوا الْقَطْرَ مِنَ السَّمَاءِ وَلَوْلاَ الْبَهَائِمُ لَمْ يُمْطَرُوا
>
> *"Immorality never appears among a people to such an extent that they commit it openly, but plagues and diseases that were never known among the predecessors will spread among them. They do not cheat in weights and measures but they will be stricken with famine, severe calamity, and the oppression of their rulers. They do not withhold the Zakāh of their wealth, but rain will be withheld from the sky, and were it not for animals, no rain would fall on them."*[156]

Sins deteriorate one's physical capabilities. Ibn al-Qayyim reasons:

> *"This is because a Mu'min's strength is sourced from his heart, the stronger his heart, the stronger the body. Even if the sinner's body is strong, he will be let down and deceived by it when he needs it most. Look at how the powerful physiques of the Persians and Romans let them down when they needed them most and were crushed by the Muslims due to the strength of the latter's bodies and hearts."*[157]

When Allāh decrees for the nations of Gog and Magog (*Ya'jūj* and *Ma'jūj*) to wreak havoc on Earth, the combined force of humanity will not be able to stop them. People will be too feeble because of rampant immorality. Concerning this prophecy, our mother Zainab (raḍiy Allāhu ʿanhā) asked the Messenger ﷺ:

---

[155] Al-Qur'ān 44:25-28

[156] Ibn Mājah, on the authority of ʿAbdullāh b. ʿUmar (raḍiy Allāhu ʿanhu)

[157] *Al-Dā' wa al-Dawā'* – Ibn al-Qayyim

> يا رَسُولَ اللَّهِ أَنَهْلِكُ وَفِينَا الصَّالِحُونَ قَالَ، نَعَمْ، إِذَا كَثُرَ الْخَبَثُ
>
> *"Allāh's Messenger! Shall we be destroyed though amongst us there are pious people?" He said, "Yes,* ***if vice becomes rampant.****"*[158]

Your Suffering is Distressing to Him

It was never the mission of our beloved Messenger ﷺ to make our lives difficult, but to guide us to what is best, even if we convince ourselves otherwise. In fact, the Messenger's ﷺ manifesto that pervaded the oldest scriptures is captured in the Qur'ān:

> الَّذِينَ يَتَّبِعُونَ الرَّسُولَ النَّبِيَّ الْأُمِّيَّ الَّذِي يَجِدُونَهُ مَكْتُوبًا عِندَهُمْ فِي التَّوْرَاةِ وَالْإِنجِيلِ يَأْمُرُهُم بِالْمَعْرُوفِ وَيَنْهَاهُمْ عَنِ الْمُنكَرِ وَيُحِلُّ لَهُمُ الطَّيِّبَاتِ وَيُحَرِّمُ عَلَيْهِمُ الْخَبَائِثَ وَيَضَعُ عَنْهُمْ إِصْرَهُمْ وَالْأَغْلَالَ الَّتِي كَانَتْ عَلَيْهِمْ ۚ فَالَّذِينَ آمَنُوا بِهِ وَعَزَّرُوهُ وَنَصَرُوهُ وَاتَّبَعُوا النُّورَ الَّذِي أُنزِلَ مَعَهُ ۙ أُولَٰئِكَ هُمُ الْمُفْلِحُونَ
>
> *Those who follow the Messenger, the unlettered Prophet, whom they find written in what they have of the Torah and the Gospel, who enjoins upon them what is right and forbids them what is wrong and makes lawful for them the good things and prohibits for them the evil and* ***relieves them of their burden and the shackles which were upon them.***[159]

The lawful is beneficial, and the unlawful detrimental. Read that, *'if he were to obey you in many things, you would suffer for it,'*[160] then read *'your suffering is distressing to him; he is deeply concerned for you; he is gentle and merciful to the believers.'*[161] Now let us ask ourselves, if my suffering causes the Messenger distress, how could obedience to his guidance possibly be the cause of my distress? It is the essence of comfort and rescue. The Messenger ﷺ was so desperate for our deliverance from that distress that he exclaimed he was:

---

[158] *Ṣaḥīḥ* Bukhārī and Muslim, on the authority of Zainab (raḍiy Allāhu ʿanhā)
[159] Al-Qur'ān 7:157
[160] Al-Qur'ān 49:7
[161] Al-Qur'ān 9:128

> *"Like that of a man who came to some people and said, 'I have seen with my own eyes the enemy forces.'"*

Heedless of his warning, he took off his clothes, simply to draw their attention to him, so that he can warn them of what awaits. He continues:

> وَإِنِّي أَنَا النَّذِيرُ الْعُرْيَانُ فَالنَّجَا النَّجَاءَ. فَأَطَاعَتْهُ طَائِفَةٌ فَأَدْلَجُوا عَلَى مَهْلِهِمْ فَنَجَوْا، وَكَذَّبَتْهُ طَائِفَةٌ فَصَبَّحَهُمُ الْجَيْشُ فَاجْتَاحَهُمْ
>
> *"I am a naked warner [to you] so save yourself, save yourself! A group of them obeyed him and went out at night, slowly and stealthily and were safe, while another group did not believe him and thus the army took them in the morning and destroyed them."*[162]

The notion that we can do and believe whatever we like is much like insects swarming towards a furious flame, mesmerised by its lure and temptation, but oblivious to its heat and devastation. The Messenger of Allāh ﷺ makes an earnest effort to keep us clear of the flame, grabbing us by his blessed hands and struggling to take us out of the blaze:

> وَأَنَا آخِذٌ بِحُجَزِكُمْ عَنِ النَّارِ وَأَنْتُمْ تَفَلَّتُونَ مِنْ يَدِي
>
> *"I am going to hold you back from fire, but you are slipping from my hand."*[163]

May Allāh's peace and blessings be upon our beloved master, Muḥammad ﷺ. So fortunate is his ummah, may we be ransomed for him. Besides his way, worldly happiness and freedom and eternal salvation are unattainable. Besides the light Allāh gives, there is simply no light. And all praise and thanks are due to Allāh.

---

[162] *Ṣaḥīḥ* Bukhārī, on the authority of Abū Mūsa (raḍiy Allāhu ʿanhu)

[163] *Ṣaḥīḥ* Muslim, on the authority of Jābir b. ʿAbdullāh (raḍiy Allāhu ʿanhu)

ALLĀH'S GREAT FAVOUR

From the outset of *Sūrat al-Ḥujurāt,* we are reminded that Allāh sent us a Messenger; defined our social structures and lines of conditional and unconditional obedience; elucidated the path to truth (*Rushd*); warned us of its impairers; addressed their behaviour, then made this path beloved to the People of Īmān. He gave us what we *need*, made it beloved to our hearts, and then rewarded us for it.

Verse 8

فَضْلًا مِّنَ اللَّهِ وَنِعْمَةً ۚ وَاللَّهُ عَلِيمٌ حَكِيمٌ

It is a great favour from Allāh and a blessing. Allāh is All-Knowing, All-Wise.[164]

Where did all of these countless blessings and privileges emerge from?

'It is a great favour from Allāh and a blessing, from the One Who possesses full and perfect knowledge. The One, the Almighty, Most Wise, who Knows those who deserve to receive the boundless gift of guidance and those who deserve otherwise. He is Wise in His words, actions, legislations, and decrees.'[165]

A Great Favour (Faḍl) against Equity (ʿAdl)

What is the difference between *Faḍl* and *ʿAdl*? *ʿAdl* is equity or justice, a magnanimous divine concept and characteristic. It is to give tit-for-tat; to give or receive exactly what is warranted. Allāh will punish by His *ʿAdl*. To live a long life whilst renouncing the cause of one's existence, Allāh, is to be neglected and eternally end up in Hell. This is *ʿAdl* in its most complete sense. But when Allāh bestows, rewards and overlooks or forgives sin, it is through His favour (*Faḍl*). If we were to be dealt with equitably after sin, we would deservedly be ruined not just for the nature of our misdeeds, but for the exaltedness of He Whom we chose to disobey:

[164] Al-Qur'ān 49:8
[165] *Jāmiʿ al-Bayān fī Ta'wīl al-Qur'ān* – Imām al-Ṭabarī

> وَلَوْ يُؤَاخِذُ اللَّهُ النَّاسَ بِمَا كَسَبُوا مَا تَرَكَ عَلَىٰ ظَهْرِهَا مِن دَابَّةٍ وَلَٰكِن يُؤَخِّرُهُمْ إِلَىٰ أَجَلٍ مُّسَمًّى فَإِذَا جَاءَ أَجَلُهُمْ فَإِنَّ اللَّهَ كَانَ بِعِبَادِهِ بَصِيرًا
>
> *If Allāh were to take mankind to task for what they have earned, He would not leave a single creature crawling on it, but He is deferring them until a specified time. Then, when their time comes, Allāh sees His slaves!.*[166]

A judge once asked a claimant, *"Do you want me to judge by 'Adl or what is better?"* The claimant asked, *"And in a Court of Justice, what is better than 'Adl?"* The judge replied, *"Faḍl."*, to which the claimant asked, *"And what is the difference?"* The judge said, *"'Adl is to take the right due to you, but Faḍl is to relinquish your claim and forgive the one who has wronged you."*[167] And to Allāh belong the most exalted examples.

Ponder on Islām and its legislations. Nothing that Allāh obligated upon us benefits Him in the slightest. He is the Almighty, the All-Wise, and the All-Powerful. He was such before everything in existence and He will continue to be thus after we die. Our obedience does not increase Him in any of this. What He obligated on us is equivalently an obligation on the rest of society. For instance, whilst Allāh commands us not to steal or to trespass the inviolable rights of others as individuals, He likewise commands millions of others to not steal from you or to trespass your inviolabile rights. Being protected from harm takes priority over indulging in it. We therefore benefit from a thing being made Ḥarām before our engaging in it is even confirmed as Ḥarām.

Focus on the following nuance. Since *we* are the direct beneficiaries of what is Ḥalāl and what is Ḥarām, we are effectively already receiving our wage (i.e., the benefit). After such 'benefits', the logical expectation – if the divine transaction was one of *'Adl* – is no further renumeration. But, as it stands, Allāh, through His legislation, gives and then rewards on top of what He gives. It is, therefore, entirely out of Allāh's *Faḍl* (rather than *'Adl*) that He rewards us for our obedience, or else we would solely deserve the benefit brought about by the legislation itself and nothing further.[168]

When the prophets called their people to Allāh's worship, their people generally rejected their call. However, almost all the prophets we know of told their people, *"I do not ask you for any payment. My payment is only from the Lord of the worlds."*[169] The prophets were well aware that their people would not pay for what they rejected

---

[166] Al-Qur'ān 35:45
[167] *Tafsīr al-Ḥujurāt* – Sheikh Muḥammad Metwalī al-Sha'rāwī
[168] *Tafsīr al-Ḥujurāt* – Sheikh Muḥammad Metwalī al-Sha'rāwī
[169] Al-Qur'ān 26:164 (one of many examples)

when offered to them free of charge! But it is as if they were telling their people, *"Since I am calling you to what is entirely for your benefit, I would naturally deserve payment for it, but the magnitude of that benefit I am bringing you is so great that none, save Allāh, can afford to pay for it."*[170]

The Indispensability of News and its Abuse

One must briefly reflect on why what is today considered a mundane pastime – reporting news – has been surrounded by some of Islām's heftiest concepts and realisations. Maybe today's inordinate accessibility to news and participation in conveying it has caused many to belittle its own significance and bearing.

News in and of itself is *indispensable*. The link between this Earth and the Heavens was established through the intermediary of 'news'. No human has seen what is beyond the visible cosmos. We were *informed*, and we trusted those who informed us. Contrary to what atheists pontificate, news *can* establish irrefutable truths when it is not contradicted by philosophical certainties. There is plenty that believers and even atheists regard as irrefutable truths, living by them and committing their lives to them purely through news they received from trustworthy sources who themselves have 'seen'. The difference is that believers acknowledge revelation ('news') as one of the devices of knowledge, whilst injudicious atheists deny it, despite *themselves* never *observing* many of the *truths* they themselves believe in.[171]

Messengers convey information about Allāh and about His will:

> نَبِّئْ عِبَادِي أَنِّي أَنَا الْغَفُورُ الرَّحِيمُ
>
> *Tell My slaves (convey the news [naba'] to them) that I am the Ever-Forgiving, the Most Merciful.*[172]

The Qur'ān contains news of Allāh and His sublime Names and Attributes; news of the previous nations and those that follow, and news of the creation of the Heavens and the Earth, the Angels, the Prophets and Messengers, the Day of Resurrection, Paradise, and the Hellfire. Several tools exist for establishing veracity, but *trust* is recognised as one of the most powerful. Trust (the audible) eclipses one's own visual observation (the visual) that can easily be tainted by perception or deception. Not a single human being questioned the immaculate integrity of the Messenger of Allāh ﷺ

---

170 *Tafsīr al-Ḥujurāt* – Sheikh Muḥammad Metwalī al-Shaʿrāwī

171 Including the unobservable philosophical concepts they use as the premise to their arguments.

172 Al-Qur'ān 15:49

prior to his Prophethood. Besides the linguistic miracle that debilitated the greatest Arab linguists and the cosmic, scientific, and specific miracles that fortified his message, his own unblemished trustworthiness is one of the greatest testimonies to his message.

Our eyes recognise that he came with something superior in its essence. Logic, too, dictates that a man who never dared lie about a mundane matter, based on the testimony of his enemies, would never tell a lie about Allāh. What, then, is the likelihood of his insisting on a lie that would bring him immense suffering and inordinate personal sacrifice? He was besieged, exiled and fought. On top of this, he gave credit of the truth he had to other than himself.[173]

As humans, we instinctually enjoy one another's news. Allāh created us with the tendency to live as tight clusters. Our strength as humans is through our communities. Today, the proliferation of news is unlike ever before. It has become a booming business, meticulously designed to catch your attention and concern. It is manufactured to correspond with precisely what you want to hear and disseminate. A report emerging from any end of the Earth can change another. News is today's uncrowned king, terrifying people on every level.

Its extent, combined with the human tendency to proliferate without scrutiny, has deformed truths beyond recognition. In his *Muqaddimah*, Ibn Khaldūn reasons that scrutinising news is rare and tiresome, and that ignorance comes hand in hand with conveying it and blindly imitating others (*Taqlīd*).

Upon today's news, people will interpret their past and define their future. Combined with its impact when consumed and proliferated, much of the news today is manufactured by industries with ulterior motives and vested interests and spun by oligarchs who profiteer from the demise of others. Today, even petty people are trusted to give the news. The Prophet ﷺ said:

> سَيَأْتِي عَلَى النَّاسِ سَنَوَاتٌ خَدَّاعَاتٌ يُصَدَّقُ فِيهَا الْكَاذِبُ وَيُكَذَّبُ فِيهَا الصَّادِقُ وَيُؤْتَمَنُ فِيهَا الْخَائِنُ وَيُخَوَّنُ فِيهَا الأَمِينُ وَيَنْطِقُ فِيهَا الرُّوَيْبِضَةُ قِيلَ وَمَا الرُّوَيْبِضَةُ قَالَ الرَّجُلُ التَّافِهُ فِي أَمْرِ الْعَامَّةِ
>
> *"'There will come to the people years of treachery, when the liar will be regarded as honest, and the honest man will be regarded as a liar; the traitor will be regarded as faithful, and the faithful man will be regarded as a traitor; and the Ruwaybidah will decide matters.' It was said: 'Who are the Ruwaybidah?' He said: 'Vile and base men who control [or speak about] the affairs of the people.'"*[174]

---

[173] For more evidence of Prophethood, see *al-Nabā' al-'Aẓīm* – 'Abdullāh Drāz

[174] Ibn Mājah, on the authority of Abu Hurairah (raḍiy Allāhu 'anhu)

Technically, *lying* is to distort realities knowingly or unknowingly. Of the two, the former is more blameworthy. However, conveying news without verification, even if done 'innocently', can easily lead one to later lie intentionally in order to defend their credibility when others discover the falsity of their report.

There are few vices Allāh reproaches in the Qur'ān more than lying. Its atrociousness has always been recognised by Muslims and non-Muslims alike. Soldiers of ancient Rome could be *cudgelled* (beaten with a stick) to death for falsifying evidence or lying under oath. Being a liar is recognisably one of the worst attributes a person can be known for. Befitting our discussion, fabricating lies is of the few vices that precludes a person's label of *Īmān*. Allāh says:

> إِنَّمَا يَفْتَرِي الْكَذِبَ الَّذِينَ لَا يُؤْمِنُونَ بِآيَاتِ اللَّهِ وَأُولَٰئِكَ هُمُ الْكَاذِبُونَ
>
> *It is only those who do not have Īmān in the Āyāt of Allāh, who fabricate falsehood, and it is they who are liars.*[175]

Al-Ḥujurāt maintains that a person shares guilt by *believing* the account of a liar. What then of the guilt of the one who creates the lie to begin with? Our mother 'Ā'ishah (raḍiy Allāhu 'anhā) used to say that a man would lie in the presence of the Messenger ﷺ and the Messenger would continue holding a type of resentment towards that person until he heard of that person turning back and repenting.[176]

Besides the individual's trustworthiness, lying can fuel division, conflict, bloodletting, and the breaking up of families. 'Uthmān (raḍiy Allāhu 'anhu) was murdered on the basis of a lie, and the devastating war between the companions was peddled and fuelled by liars outside of Madīnah.

Ibn Taymiyyah reasons that *truthfulness* is the foundation of *all* good deeds, whilst lying is the foundation of *all* sins. The distinction of man over animals is through the former's rationale. Rationale then culminates in composed speech in the form of performatives (*Inshā'*) or constatives (*khabar*). The latter describe the world around us, for example 'the sky is blue'. These descriptions can be affirmed or denied and can thus be changed by lies. Performatives are used to carry out an action and cannot be affirmed or falsified such as to say 'I apologise'.[177] Constatives can only be established through truthfulness and honesty and are also distorted by the opposite. Constatives are, furthermore, the root of performatives, and form the backbone of knowledge,

---

[175] Al-Qur'ān 16:105

[176] Al-Tirmithī and Aḥmad on the authority of 'Ā'ishah (raḍiy Allāhu 'anhā)

[177] With performatives, the speaker does not describe the world, but changes it to say "I apologise for my behaviour." This form of speech is based on realities (or distortions) established by constatives.

whilst performatives form the backbone of action. With this in mind, it can easily be seen how sin (action) can result from distorted knowledge.

Using this description, Ibn Taymiyyah argues that since the ability to form constatives is what differentiates man from animal and gives the former rationale, a liar's behaviour is worse than an animal. Additionally, the distinguishing characteristic between a *Mu'min* and a *Munāfiq* is truthfulness.[178] Truthfulness of intention is likewise what distinguishes a sincere person from a show-off, and showing off is a symptom of hypocrisy. And Allāh knows best.

The drive to sin usually happens during moments of distorted reality. This is because Hell is still there, Paradise is still there and Allāh and His inscribing Angels are still watching and recording. But at the *moment of sin*, something in one's self causes one to belie that knowledge as if it does not exist, leading him or her to sin. The Prophet ﷺ said:

> إِيَّاكُمْ وَالْكَذِبَ، فَإِنَّ الْكَذِبَ يَهْدِي إِلَى الْفُجُورِ، وَإِنَّ الْفُجُورَ يَهْدِي إِلَى النَّارِ، وَمَا يَزَالُ الرَّجُلُ يَكْذِبُ، وَيَتَحَرَّى الْكَذِبَ، حَتَّى يُكْتَبَ عِنْدَ اللَّهِ كَذَّابًا
>
> *"Avoid [you people] lying, for lying leads to wickedness and wickedness leads to Hell, and if a man continues to lie and makes lying his object, he will be recorded as a liar before Allāh."*[179]

Al-Ḥujurāt is full of open and subtle references to truthfulness and the harm of its opposite. Open lies do not only lead to conflict and guilt, but tear apart the ties of brotherhood. Inner lies defy one's *Taqwā*, contradict with claims to *Īmān* and are ultimately exposed – as we will discover in **'The Reality of Īmān'**. And Allāh is the source of success.

---

[178] See *Majmū'at al-Fatāwa* – Ibn Taymiyyah

[179] *Ṣaḥīḥ* Bukhārī and Muslim on the authority of ʿAbdullāh b. Mas'ūd (raḍiy Allāhu ʿanhu)

WHO BROUGHT THE FALSE REPORT TO THE PROPHET?

The unmatched style and power of the Qur'ān is that it seamlessly addresses past events whilst simultaneously establishing eternal lessons and principles. In the first six verses of *al-Ḥujurāt* alone no less than three separate accounts are specifically addressed without names, dates, nor unnecessary details.

It was narrated on the authority of Umm Salamah, the Prophet's ﷺ wife, that the verse of verification was revealed when the Prophet ﷺ sent a companion by the name of al-Walīd b. ʿUqbah b. Abī Muʿayt to a tribe called Banī al-Mustaliq to collect their Zakāh at the time it was due.

Banī al-Mustaliq had already embraced Islām and there was no doubt about their certainty or devotion. They were cognisant of the due date of their Zakāh and were in fact eager to pay. It is said that they emerged from their town, possibly as a group, to either receive the Prophet's messenger or to deliver the Zakāh to the Prophet ﷺ themselves. Just as the Prophet's delegate, al-Walīd, approached, he saw the uncustomary spectacle: a sizeable and intimidating group of people bearing their arms at the borders of their town. Al-Walīd, struck by fear and suspicion, turned and headed back to Madīnah. Some exegetes reason that what exacerbated this sentiment was some pre-Islāmic hostility that existed between him and members of Banī al-Mustaliq.

Al-Walīd returned to the Prophet ﷺ, informing him that Banī al-Mustaliq had emerged intending to kill him and were, by extension, intending to prevent paying their Zakāh! The Messenger ﷺ was infuriated and some narrations indicate that he considered dispatching a contingent of soldiers. Others mention that the Prophet did actually dispatch Khālid b. al-Walīd (raḍiy Allāhu ʿanhu) to verify the account. Whilst at the periphery of their town, Khālid sent in scouts to investigate. On their return, they informed Khālid that Banī al-Mustaliq were in fact routinely raising the Adhān and praying the Ṣalāh at its prescribed time. They were undoubtedly still committed to Islām.

Through the Prophet's investigation, the Messenger ﷺ was able to confirm their real intentions through either Khālid or the physical coming of the tribe to him. Banī al-Mustaliq asked the Prophet ﷺ why the initial delegate (al-Walīd b. ʿUqbah) rushed to leave before collecting the Zakāh, fearing that it was the Prophet who ordered him to return. The tribe continued pleading their case with the Prophet until it was clear that they intended no harm and were extremely committed to Islām and to their financial duties. Recall the verse:

> *If he were to obey you in many things, you would suffer for it...*

Had the Messenger ﷺ believed the account that Banī al-Mustaliq had left Islām and refused to pay the Zakāh, a war may have resulted that would have spilt inviolable blood and wealth, and some may have been punished by Allāh. Like Banī Tamīm mentioned in the previous section, Banī al-Mustaliq came to the Prophet for a similar reason but surrounded by different circumstances. This may be why the two accounts are mentioned side by side. Allāh thus revealed these verses guiding the ummah then and today on the correct etiquette for engaging with collectives of people and upon receiving news in general.

Is a Companion Being Labelled a Fāsiq?

The first question that may come to mind is, does this mean al-Walīd (raḍiy Allāhu ʿanhu), a companion of the Prophet ﷺ, can be called a *Fāsiq*? This is considering such a label's implications on honesty and integrity, against the established trustworthiness of all companions. As a matter of fact, the *Mufassirūn* have agreed that this is *not* the case. What occurred from al-Walīd was nothing more than speculation, and nothing implies that he either desired to cause harm or intended on telling a lie. It is farfetched and unjust to label al-Walīd a *Fāsiq* since he was mistaken in his judgement, and a person who makes a genuine mistake cannot be called a *Fāsiq*. It was further narrated that the Prophet ﷺ merely said to al-Walīd:

> التَّبْيِينُ مِنَ اللَّهِ والعَجَلَةُ مِنَ الشَّيْطانِ
>
> *"Scrutiny is from Allāh and haste is from the Shayṭān."*[180]

Scrutiny allows a person time to reflect, according to Ibn al-Jawzī, and an opportunity to consider, compare, and contrast the different circumstances underpinning an account. It becomes as if a person has consulted himself, or carried out a personal *Shūrā*. He likens this to bread, the quality of which depends on the time it is left to ferment; the longer, the better.[181] Opinion left to ferment is superior to that which is expressed instantly. The word *'Aql*, though it contextually refers to the intellect, is linguistically sourced from *'what restrains from obnoxious action and speech.'*[182] The purpose of one's intellect is thus to restrain a person from doing what should not be done in haste. Haste is the reason for many of our misinformed opinions, confutations and resulting enormous regrets.

---

[180] *Mursal* narration on the authority of al-Ḥasan al-Baṣrī

[181] *Sayd al-Khātir* – Ibn al-Jawzī

[182] *Mu'jam Maqāyīs al-Lughah* – Aḥmad b. Fāris al-Qazwīnī

Nowhere did the Prophet ﷺ reprimand al-Walīd or order him to repent for what he did. In fact, it was completely out of the ordinary for any tribe to come out to receive the person collecting the Zakāh. Ask yourself, what would the taxman think if he saw the debtor waiting on his doorstep with a weapon in his hand when he had felt unwelcome to begin with? Ibn ʿĀshūr speculates that the leaders of Banī al-Mustaliq tried to deter al-Walīd's entry on purpose. This was not to prevent their Zakāh, but they felt that his entry would arouse resentment among their laity and remind them of old blood, especially when they saw him taking their money! Ironically, their intentions in that case were to prevent conflict rather than to cause it.

All of the Prophet's ﷺ companions are trustworthy by the agreement of the scholars of Islām. A companion encompasses he or she who saw the Prophet ﷺ, and believed in him or those who lived around him and supported him. Even if we take the latter, most conservative opinion that a companion is someone who lived directly around him and supported him, this will still include the vast majority of companions we know by name. And Allāh knows best.

SECTION 3: CONFLICT RESOLUTION AND RECONCILING BETWEEN MUSLIMS

Allāh has now warned us about the news conveyed by the *Fāsiq*, both the habitual liar and the one who is indifferent about major or lesser sins. In the next few āyāt of *Sūrah al-Ḥujurāt* Allāh teaches us the particular and natural repercussions of ignoring such advice: strife, conflict, and disunity. Had the Prophet ﷺ taken action upon hearing the news about Banī al-Mustaliq, he would have fought them. Unverified news and miscommunication are of the greatest causes of conflict. In the event that fake news *is* nonetheless spread, Allāh the All-Merciful guides us to the resolution of the ensuing conflict leaving no eventuality excluded:

Verses 9-10

> وَإِن طَائِفَتَانِ مِنَ الْمُؤْمِنِينَ اقْتَتَلُوا فَأَصْلِحُوا بَيْنَهُمَا ۖ فَإِن بَغَتْ إِحْدَاهُمَا عَلَى الْأُخْرَىٰ فَقَاتِلُوا الَّتِي تَبْغِي حَتَّىٰ تَفِيءَ إِلَىٰ أَمْرِ اللَّهِ ۚ فَإِن فَاءَتْ فَأَصْلِحُوا بَيْنَهُمَا بِالْعَدْلِ وَأَقْسِطُوا ۖ إِنَّ اللَّهَ يُحِبُّ الْمُقْسِطِينَ ۞ إِنَّمَا الْمُؤْمِنُونَ إِخْوَةٌ فَأَصْلِحُوا بَيْنَ أَخَوَيْكُمْ ۚ وَاتَّقُوا اللَّهَ لَعَلَّكُمْ تُرْحَمُونَ
>
> *If two parties of the Mu'minūn fight, make peace between them. But if one of them attacks the other unjustly, fight the attackers until they revert to Allāh's command.*

> *If they revert, make peace between them with justice, and be even-handed. Allāh loves those who are even-handed. The Mu'minūn are brothers, so make peace between your brothers and have Taqwā of Allāh so that hopefully you will gain mercy.*[183]

The worst form of unverified reporting is that which is spread by groups of people about other groups. This is because scrutinising such reports is more difficult than scrutinising those concerning individuals. Sometimes fights will break out even before one has a chance to reconcile. As far as undoing the damage, regret in such circumstances is futile.[184] Thus Allāh commands the *Mu'minūn* to try their best at pre-empting conflict through reconciliation by providing advice, reminders, guidance, and fair judgement until one of the two parties crosses the limits and insists on its offence. In all cases, this intervention is to be overshadowed by Allāh's *Taqwā* and His preference, not our personal biases, prejudices, or irritations.

Verse 9

> وَإِن طَائِفَتَانِ مِنَ الْمُؤْمِنِينَ اقْتَتَلُوا فَأَصْلِحُوا بَيْنَهُمَا ۖ فَإِن بَغَتْ إِحْدَاهُمَا عَلَى الْأُخْرَىٰ فَقَاتِلُوا الَّتِي تَبْغِي حَتَّىٰ تَفِيءَ إِلَىٰ أَمْرِ اللَّهِ ۚ فَإِن فَاءَتْ فَأَصْلِحُوا بَيْنَهُمَا بِالْعَدْلِ وَأَقْسِطُوا ۖ إِنَّ اللَّهَ يُحِبُّ الْمُقْسِطِينَ
>
> *If two parties of the Mu'minūn fight, make peace between them. But if one of them attacks the other unjustly, fight the attackers until they revert to Allāh's command. If they revert, make peace between them with justice, and be even-handed. Allāh loves those who are even-handed.*[185]

If two parties from the people of Īmān fight, then make peace between them by inviting them to judge by the Book of Allāh and to be contented with what it contains, both for them and against them. This is how to reconcile *justly*.[186] This invitation can assume the form of offering advice (*Nuṣḥ*), by inviting them to return to Allāh's

[183] Al-Qur'ān 49:9-10
[184] *Tafsīr al-Taḥrīr wa al-Tanwīr* – Ibn ʿĀshūr
[185] Al-Qur'ān 49:9
[186] *Jāmiʿ al-Bayān fī Ta'wīl al-Qur'ān* – Imām al-Ṭabarī

command directly or to the terms of an agreement previously signed between them such as a contract or a truce. Obeying such agreements is also part of returning to Allāh's command.[187] Allāh says:

> يا أَيُّها الَّذينَ آمَنوا أَوفوا بِالعُقودِ
>
> *You who have Īmān! Fulfil your contracts.*[188]

'If a conflicting party refuses to comply when invited to judge by the Book of Allāh, containing what is due to them of rights and what is due on them of duties, and transgresses the justice that Allāh has afforded His creatures whilst the other responds, 'fight the attackers.' Fight them 'until they revert to Allāh's command'; the command that Allāh has provided in the Qur'ān to provide judgement between His creatures.'[189]

'If they revert, make peace between them with justice ('Adl), and be even-handed (Qisṭ).'[190] If the transgressing party that you fight re-evaluates its position and becomes satisfied with Allāh's judgement in His Book, then make peace between the two parties with justice, dealing fairly between both.

Some have suggested that *'Adl* and *Qisṭ* are synonymous. In such a case, the repetition of *Qisṭ* is added for emphasis. This would mean that the one restoring justice by addressing what the two parties did to one another (i.e., restoring usurped rights and carrying out retribution for any wrongdoing), should do so *justly.*[191] Others have differentiated between the meanings of *'Adl* and *Qisṭ*. The *Muqsiṭ* (from *Qisṭ*) is the one who gives every single person their due, in an apparent and visible way. In this case, *Qisṭ* is more specific than *'Adl* as it is a type of justice that makes evident rights and dues to those watching the reconciliation. From it comes the word *'Qisṭās'*, which is the iron rod that holds up traditional scales. Scales are used to physically display justice and fairness in that which is weighed. When the two plates are finely balanced, there is equity, and when one hangs below the other, there is inequity, visible to the dealing party.[192]

This would mean that the second process is about making justice apparent, distinguishing clearly between culprit and victim. It is, in a way, a firmer approach, ensuring that when hostilities end and emotions are no longer raw, the matter is

---

[187] *Anwār al-Tanzīl* – al-Baidāwī
[188] Al-Qur'ān 5:1
[189] *Jāmi' al-Bayān fī Ta'wīl al-Qur'ān* – Imām al-Ṭabarī
[190] Al-Qur'ān 49:9
[191] *Tafsīr al-Qur'ān al-'Aẓīm* – Ibn Kathīr
[192] *Al-Furūq al-Lughawiyyah* – Abu Hilāl al-'Askarī

settled once and for all, justice and rights are restored and the original dispute is not repeated.

Despite the start of the verse linguistically occurring in the past tense (literally, *'If two parties of the Mu'minūn* ***have*** *fought'*), it should be understood as, *'if two parties of the Mu'minūn* ***desire*** *to fight'*. This is akin to Allāh saying, *'You who have Īmān! When you get up to do Ṣalāh* (read literally 'when you have **gotten up** to do Ṣalāh [in the past tense]'), *wash your faces and your hands...'*[193] Obviously, *Wuḍū'* takes place before *Ṣalāh*, and thus the linguistic dictates are of a future tense nature, i.e., when you *intend* on performing *Ṣalāh*. The verse of *al-Ḥujurāt* therefore tells us that a fight should be prevented when others sense it brewing and before it even has a chance to transpire.[194]

The word *'Ṭā'ifah'* refers to a group of people in the linguistically singular form. When Allāh refers to the involved groups, He uses the dual form 'two parties' (*Ṭā'ifatān*). Yet when He refers to the fighting, He uses the plural form (*Iqtatalū*), not the dual form (*Iqtatalatā*). Some have suggested that this may be because war is usually declared by the heads of the two parties (the dual), but when it rages, it affects and involves the collective.[195] Yet more profound is that when Allāh refers to making peace He goes back to using the dual form, *'make peace between them [both]'* (*fa aṣliḥū baynahumā*). The implied directive for reconciliation is that the peace maker should target those very two heads or leaders who declared war or decided to initiate the problem for the collective to stop fighting. The mediator does not necessarily need to reconcile between every individual involved.[196]

'Fighting' the aggressing party, according to some, means to coerce them (*al-daf*) to fair judgement. Qatādah said:

> *"It is not as those with erroneous beliefs, innovations, and lies against Allāh and His Book said, that 'it is a dispensation to kill a Muslim', for Allāh sanctified and protected the Muslim, to the extent that you cannot but think good about your brother [let alone fight them]. Allāh says in the verse immediately following this one: 'The Mu'minūn are brothers.'"*[197]

[193] Al-Qur'ān 5:6
[194] *Tafsīr al-Taḥrīr wa al-Tanwīr* – Ibn ʿĀshūr
[195] *Ḥawl Tafsīr Sūrat al-Ḥujurāt* – ʿAbdullāh Sirāj al-Dīn
[196] *Tafsīr al-Ḥujurāt* – Muḥammad Metwalī al-Shaʿrāwī
[197] *Jāmiʿ al-Bayān fī Ta'wīl al-Qur'ān* – Imām al-Ṭabarī

Protecting and Maintaining Harmonious Nations

Although the concept of making peace is general, the action of 'fighting' the aggressing party is primarily directed at the Head of State after every effort has been made to restore the right of the oppressed. Using force to maintain law and order is always exclusively a political state's dispensation. The fact that Allāh addresses the leader of the Muslim community reinforces the idea that *Sūrat al-Ḥujurāt* was revealed at a time when Muslims were dominant and in charge, necessitating legislation to govern social order. As such, this legislation is primarily intended to govern states and armies with what they should do to maintain harmonious societies.

Besides fighting, there is no doubt that the spirit of the message applies in every instance of conflict. In fact, it shows that if ordinary individuals are able to reconcile before state involvement, they have carried out a good deed so enormous and rewardable that it would have otherwise religiously escalated to state-level.

The drastic measure of fighting the aggressing party emphasises the importance of maintaining societal harmony and brotherhood when in every other situation it is entirely prohibited. The *only reason* they are fought is because they have gotten out of control. As a group, they cannot otherwise be easily restrained.

Notice that Allāh referred to the two fighting parties as *'Mu'minūn'* in spite of their fighting. Many have used this verse to prove that a major sin does not invalidate a person's Īmān. This is unlike the attitude held by many heretic groups who excommunicate people from Islām for trivial matters, let alone major sins. The Prophet ﷺ once delivered a sermon with his grandson Ḥasan b. ʿAlī (raḍiy Allāhu ʿanhu) sitting on his lap. Looking at him once and at the congregation again, the Prophet said:

> إِنَّ ابْنِي هَذَا سَيِّدٌ وَلَعَلَّ اللَّهَ أَنْ يُصْلِحَ بِهِ بَيْنَ فِئَتَيْنِ عَظِيمَتَيْنِ مِنَ الْمُسْلِمِينَ
>
> *"This son of mine is a Sayyid (i.e. a noble) and Allāh may make peace through him between two huge groups of* **Muslims***."*[198]

Through Ḥasan b. ʿAlī (raḍiy Allāhu ʿanhu), Allāh reconciled between the people of Greater Syria and those of Iraq after the colossal events between the *'two huge groups of Muslims.'*[199] Our love of one companion or another, or indeed the family of the Messenger of Allāh ﷺ, should never lead us to excommunicate those who may have differed with them because of their Islāmic judgement and understanding. By the

[198] *Ṣaḥīḥ* Bukhārī on the authority of Abu Bakr (raḍiy Allāhu ʿanhu)
[199] *Tafsīr al-Qur'ān al-ʿAẓīm* – Ibn Kathīr

Prophet's testimony, they were both Muslims despite their fighting. It is well known that in this very incident, they did exactly what Allāh ordered in the verse of *al-Ḥujurāt*, striving towards reconciliation using the Book of Allāh. It was the *Khawārij*, after claiming they would be satisfied with the judgement of the Book of Allāh, who were the first to protest against that judgement because they were instead vying for power.

'Fight the attackers' is only prescribed to the extent needed for them to return to Allāh and His Messenger's commands and is thus a limited means to an objective. That objective is to bring about their own ultimate benefit and protection. This is much like forcefully stopping a person from destroying his or herself, particularly on occasions when their anger causes them to lose their sanity or sound judgement. Such are the hallmarks of the Islāmic interdependent and altruistic community. Its members look out for one another and determine that the repercussions of being forced out of evil are much better than being given the 'freedom' to engage in it as one pleases.[200] The Messenger of Allāh ﷺ said:

> انْصُرْ أَخَاكَ ظَالِمًا أَوْ مَظْلُومًا. قُلْتُ، يَا رَسُولَ اللَّهِ، هَذَا نَصَرْتُهُ مَظْلُومًا فَكَيْفَ أَنْصُرُهُ ظَالِمًا؟ قَالَ، تَمْنَعُهُ مِنَ الظُّلْمِ، فَذَاكَ نَصْرُكَ إِيَّاهُ
>
> *"Help your brother, whether he is an oppressor or he is an oppressed one." People asked, "O Allāh's Messenger! It is all right to help him if he is oppressed, but how should we help him if he is an oppressor?" The Prophet said, "By preventing him from oppressing others."*[201]

And Allāh knows best.

---

[200] Note here that absolute, unrestricted freedom can never be an objective and is instead anarchy.
[201] *Ṣaḥīḥ* Bukhārī on the authority of Anas b. Mālik (raḍiy Allāhu ʿanhu)

THE IMPERATIVENESS OF JUSTICE

Ibn Taymiyyah (raḥimahu Allāhu) is reported to have said, *"Allāh raises the just nation, even if it is a disbelieving one, and He does not raise the oppressive nation, even if it is a believing one."* Justice is not only a religious imperative but also a universal law upon which Allāh created everything. Justice is a destination to which everything will return and is always ultimately served and restored. It governs the cosmos as it does the most subtle elements of creation. Oppression is the deformation of that equity and balance.

> وَإِن طَائِفَتَانِ مِنَ الْمُؤْمِنِينَ اقْتَتَلُوا فَأَصْلِحُوا بَيْنَهُمَا ۖ فَإِن بَغَتْ إِحْدَاهُمَا عَلَى الْأُخْرَىٰ فَقَاتِلُوا الَّتِي
> تَبْغِي حَتَّىٰ تَفِيءَ إِلَىٰ أَمْرِ اللَّهِ ۚ فَإِن فَاءَتْ فَأَصْلِحُوا بَيْنَهُمَا بِالْعَدْلِ وَأَقْسِطُوا ۖ إِنَّ اللَّهَ يُحِبُّ
> الْمُقْسِطِينَ
>
> *If two parties of the believers fight, make peace between them. But if one of them attacks the other unjustly, fight the attackers until they revert to Allāh's command. If they revert, make peace between them with justice, and be even-handed. Allāh loves those who are even-handed.*[202]

The Subtle 'Expectations' in the Verse

Notice that the verses subtly indicate that the arbitrator should know what constitutes fairness before administering it in conflict resolution. The parties in conflict are also expected to submit to the justice outlined in the Book of Allāh. The arbitrator is thus required to have both knowledge of *what* constitutes fairness and impartiality relevant to the parties involved, and knowledge of *how* to apply it. Whilst the verse demonstrates that it *is* possible (albeit uncommon) that Mu'minūn will fight, it should not be possible for either of the two to outright refuse to be judged by the justice of Islām, even when those involved perceive that the judgement is against them, or has made them feel humiliated by owing something of compensation or amends.

The companion Zubair (raḍiy Allāhu ʿanhu) quarrelled with a man from the *Anṣār* because of a natural mountainous stream at a place called al-Ḥarra. They went to the Prophet ﷺ for a judgement to which he said:

---

[202] Al-Qur'ān 49:9

> *"Zubair! Irrigate [your lands] and then let the water flow to your neighbour." The Anṣāri said, "O Allāh's Messenger, is this because he (Zubair) is your cousin?" At that, the Prophet's face became red [with anger] and he said, "O Zubair! Irrigate [your land] and then withhold the water till it fills the land up to the walls and then let it flow to your neighbour."*[203]

Initially, the Prophet ﷺ gave an order encouraging Zubair (raḍiy Allāhu ʿanhu) to make a concession. When the *Anṣāri* accused the Messenger ﷺ of favouring his relative, he ruled that Zubair should instead take his legally *due* share of the water. Zubair said, "*I think the following verse was revealed concerning this incident*":

> فَلَا وَرَبِّكَ لَا يُؤْمِنُونَ حَتَّىٰ يُحَكِّمُوكَ فِيمَا شَجَرَ بَيْنَهُمْ ثُمَّ لَا يَجِدُوا فِي أَنفُسِهِمْ حَرَجًا مِّمَّا قَضَيْتَ وَيُسَلِّمُوا تَسْلِيمًا
>
> *No, by your Lord, they will not believe until they make you their judge in the disputes that break out between them, and then find no resistance within themselves to what you decide and submit themselves completely.*[204]

Notice the link between the conflicting parties acceding to the justice afforded by Islām and the first verse of the *Sūrah* which warns against putting oneself before Allāh and His Messenger ﷺ in any way. It is as if the first verse permeates every following injunction. In this case, should a fight take place and the arbitrator reminds those parties in conflict of Allāh and His Messenger ﷺ, their Īmān should encourage them to stop and submit to that judgement.

Reconciliation with Justice, above Everything Else

Allāh says:

> يَا أَيُّهَا الَّذِينَ آمَنُوا كُونُوا قَوَّامِينَ بِالْقِسْطِ شُهَدَاءَ لِلَّهِ وَلَوْ عَلَىٰ أَنفُسِكُمْ أَوِ الْوَالِدَيْنِ وَالْأَقْرَبِينَ ۚ إِن يَكُنْ غَنِيًّا أَوْ فَقِيرًا فَاللَّهُ أَوْلَىٰ بِهِمَا...

---

[203] *Ṣaḥīḥ* Bukhārī on the authority of ʿUrwa b. az-Zubair (raḍiy Allāhu ʿanhu)
[204] Al-Qur'ān 4:65

> *You who have Īmān!* ***Be upholders of justice****, bearing witness for Allāh alone, even against yourselves or your parents and relatives. Whether they are rich or poor, Allāh is well able to look after them...*[205]

Reflect for a moment on the above verse. An arbitrator must not side with the rich *because* they are rich and influential, nor with the poor *because* they are poor and have drawn empathy. Even if the sight of a rich person demanding their small dues from a poor person is frustrating, side with justice, regardless of whom it happens to be with and be just when imparting justice.

Islām's directive to arbitrators even includes not lending one of the two conflicting sides more attention than the other, nor giving either a friendlier address than the other. The verse goes further to command that one should not even side with themselves, their parents, or closest relatives if they are in the wrong. Do *everything* you can to eradicate the main culprit in preventing justice: your personal inclinations and desires (*al-Hawa*). It comes as no surprise that the aforementioned verse is one of the quotes exhibited at the main entrance of Harvard University's Department of Justice, labelled as the best justice quote.

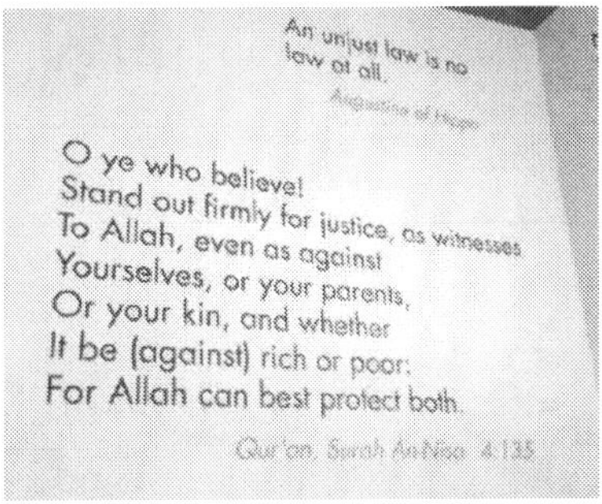

The verse continues:

> فَلَا تَتَّبِعُوا الْهَوَىٰ أَن تَعْدِلُوا...
>
> *Do not follow your own desires lest you avoid justice...*

Finally, be just in the words you choose to use. For some, anger brings out the worst of what they know, completely defaming the reputation of their opponents or finding nothing good to say about them whatsoever. For others, happiness and love

[205] Al-Qur'ān 4:135

causes them to overexaggerate their appreciation and praise, only for them to regret such words later. All of this falls short of justice.

The Prophet ﷺ said:

> إن المقسطين عند الله على منابر من نور عن يمين الرحمن – عز وجل – وكلتا يديه يمين، الذين يعدلون في حكمهم وأهليهم وما وَلُوا
>
> *"Certainly, those who were fair will be in the presence of Allāh upon pulpits of light, near the right hand of the Merciful, the Exalted, and both of His sides are right [being equal in honour]. [They are] those who practiced justice in their rulings and with their families and in all that they did."*[206]

The Challenge of Reconciling after a Fight

Refer again to the ninth verse of *al-Ḥujurāt*. Observe how in the first instance Allāh orders to *'make peace between them'*. But following one party's assault of the other and after the arbitrator compels the aggressors to the judgement of Allāh, Allāh says, *'If they revert, make peace between them with justice, and be even-handed.'* Naturally, the party that has been compelled to peace and forced to abandon its weapons or forgo their zealous offensive will feel defeated and humiliated. Therefore, the arbitrators must strive even harder to remove any grudges felt by enticing both parties to return to the brotherhood of Islām.[207]

After the considerable effort exerted towards peace, it would be extremely irritating for that arbitrator if one of the two parties were to perform an act of aggression yet again. In such circumstances, there is a chance that the second arbitration will be agreed by that incensed arbitrator with terms that oppress or disadvantage the aggressing party! The peacemaking arbitrator may well lose their impartiality, judging by their own desires (*Hawā*). They are thus reminded that *even if* they have been aggravated by that transgression, or were indeed compelled to *'fight the aggressor'*, that is no reason to forgo justice and fairness towards them if they return to the command of Allāh. And Allāh knows best.

---

[206] *Ṣaḥīḥ* Muslim on the authority of ʿAbdullāh b. ʿUmar (raḍiy Allāhu ʿanhu)
[207] *Tafsīr al-Taḥrīr wa al-Tanwīr* – Ibn ʿĀshūr

THE REAL FOUNDATION OF BROTHERHOOD

Rules are rules, as the expression goes. Generally, this means 'just obey them without asking why they exist'. In the Qur'ān, even when giving firm directives, it appeals to the hearer's soft emotions and spirits. The directive discussed previously is that, *'if two parties of the Mu'minūn fight, make peace between them [...] with justice, and be even-handed...'*[208] What follows is a directive that, more than commanding obedience, entices to an aspired way of life.

Verse 10

> إِنَّمَا الْمُؤْمِنُونَ إِخْوَةٌ فَأَصْلِحُوا بَيْنَ أَخَوَيْكُمْ ۚ وَاتَّقُوا اللَّهَ لَعَلَّكُمْ تُرْحَمُونَ
>
> ***The Mu'minūn are brothers,*** *so make peace between your brothers and have Taqwā of Allāh so that hopefully you will gain mercy.*[209]

Here, Allāh addresses the people of Īmān by saying that the Mu'minūn are siblings in religion, *'so make peace between your brothers'* if they fight by guiding them towards the command of Allāh and His Messenger ﷺ. Though 'your brothers' (*akhawayn*) occurs in the dual form, it encompasses every group of Mu'minūn who fight. *'And have Taqwā of Allāh so that hopefully you will gain mercy'* means fear Allāh by justly making peace between two believing parties involved in a dispute – as He commands. Likewise avoid sin so that Allāh will show you mercy by overlooking your previous offences. It is a promise that reaches three parties simultaneously, the one in the right, the one in the wrong, and the arbitrator.[210]

Obtain Mercy by Restoring Mercy

One may ask why Allāh specifically promises to bestow His Mercy in this instance. In the verse, the command towards *Taqwā* occurs alongside a reminder of our relationship as brethren. With that relationship in mind, *Taqwā* manifests in how to deal mercifully towards one another, restoring the natural mercy siblings have

[208] Al-Qur'ān 49:9
[209] Al-Qur'ān 49:10
[210] *Jāmi' al-Bayān fī Ta'wīl al-Qur'ān* – Imām al-Ṭabarī

towards one another.[211] Biological siblings emerge from the same womb (*Raḥim*) and mercy (*Raḥma*) comes from this root. As such, they are predisposed to be merciful towards one another. The expression *'Ikhwah'* emphatically extends that mercy to other Muslims, for they have been made your siblings, not by a womb you share, but by what is greater; the Īmān you share.

As such, if raḥma is extended to your siblings in Islām through earnest attempts at reconciling between their hearts, Allāh will consequentially show you mercy, for you reap what you sow. Show mercy and you will be shown mercy. The reality of *'Ukhuwwah'* is the direct reason (*illah*) behind the previous injunction to 'make peace'. The reason you need to make peace is because to one another you are like a unity of siblings. It further came in the linguistic form of a restrictive sentence (*Ḥaṣr*). The verse can be read, *'the Mu'minūn are* ***nothing but*** *brothers'*.

The verse does not include a statement which implies likeness (a simile) such as to say, *'the Mu'minūn are like brothers'* (*ka al-Ikhwah*), but rather, *'the Mu'minūn are brothers'*, so as not to weaken the reality of this relationship. In that sense theirs is an indivisible bond truer than one's biological bonds.[212]

Further to this, it is known and accepted that when members of families fall into dispute, the rest of the family immediately and instinctively responds. When Allāh tells us that the *'the Mu'minūn are brothers'*, it is no longer necessary to say *'so make peace between the two disputing parties'*, but *'between your brothers'*. This attracts the equivalent impulse towards reconciliation you would lend to your biological families. Both of the disputing parties are your siblings and they are, by extension, siblings of one another despite their dispute. Therefore, restore what is expected of a sibling to his sibling.[213] All this, and more, is flawlessly encapsulated in just three words, *'innama al-mu'minūna ikhwah'*.

Another perspective of *'so that you may be shown mercy'* is that addressing enmity before it flares up is a mercy for you as the mediator. This is because if you fail to make peace, each party will despise the other. You, as the mediator have no such sentiments. But if, after the confrontation, you deal kindly with either party, the other will naturally see you as having taken the side of their enemy and will begin despising you as well![214] As such, show mercy to your very selves by reconciling between your siblings.

The use of *'Innama'* meaning 'surely', 'definitely', and 'without doubt' further insists that such a reality is well-known and determined (*ma'lūmun muqarrar*). It is something that hardly needs a reminder and should certainly not come as news. Consider when Allāh speaks of the Mu'minūn of later generations supplicating for those who preceded them in Īmān:

---

[211] *Tafsīr al-Taḥrīr wa al-Tanwīr* – Ibn 'Āshūr
[212] *Tafsīr al-Taḥrīr wa al-Tanwīr* – Ibn 'Āshūr
[213] *Tafsīr al-Taḥrīr wa al-Tanwīr* – Ibn 'Āshūr
[214] *Tafsīr al-Ḥujurāt* – Muḥammad Metwalī al-Sha'rāwī

> وَالَّذِينَ جَاءُوا مِن بَعْدِهِمْ يَقُولُونَ رَبَّنَا اغْفِرْ لَنَا وَلِإِخْوَانِنَا الَّذِينَ سَبَقُونَا بِالْإِيمَانِ وَلَا تَجْعَلْ فِي قُلُوبِنَا غِلًّا لِّلَّذِينَ آمَنُوا رَبَّنَا إِنَّكَ رَءُوفٌ رَّحِيمٌ
>
> *Those who have come after them say, "Our Lord, forgive us and our brothers who preceded us in Īmān and do not put any rancour in our hearts towards those who have Īmān. Our Lord, You are All-Gentle, Most Merciful."*[215]

The verse determines that '*those who come after them **say***' not 'should say'. Such an action is anticipated or assumed due to the extraordinary strength of the relationship. If this applies to former nations, what, then, of those amongst us today? In support of this, the Prophet ﷺ used to say about his deeply intimate and inseparable companion Abu Bakr (raḍiy Allāhu ʿanhu):

> إِنَّهُ لَيْسَ مِنَ النَّاسِ أَحَدٌ أَمَنَّ عَلَيَّ فِي نَفْسِهِ وَمَالِهِ مِنْ أَبِي بَكْرِ بْنِ أَبِي قُحَافَةَ، وَلَوْ كُنْتُ مُتَّخِذًا مِنَ النَّاسِ خَلِيلاً لَاتَّخَذْتُ أَبَا بَكْرٍ خَلِيلاً، وَلَكِنْ خُلَّةُ الإِسْلَامِ أَفْضَلُ
>
> *"There is no one who had done more favour to me with his life and property than Abu Bakr b. Abi Quhafa. If I were to take a Khalīl,*[216] *I would certainly have taken Abu Bakr, but Islām's brotherhood is superior..."*[217]

Ponder over the indivisible relationship between the Messenger ﷺ and Abu Bakr (raḍiy Allāhu ʿanhu); their attachment, mutual support, encouragement, and unmatched companionship. Despite the strength and exclusivity of this bond, the Messenger ﷺ found bestowing Islām's Ukhuwwah towards Abu Bakr superior to the greatest forms of human love between friends – *Khullah*!

---

[215] Al-Qur'ān 59:10

[216] *Khalīl* – an intimate friend whose love has penetrated the depths of the heart like *Khal* (vinegar) penetrates pickles.

[217] *Ṣaḥīḥ* Bukhārī on the authority of ʿAbdullāh b. ʿAbbās (raḍiy Allāhu ʿanhu)

"You Are My Brother" is Not Just a Cliché

Ibn Kathīr reminds us of some of the narrations concerning brotherhood, such as when the Prophet ﷺ said:[218]

> دَعْوَةُ الْمَرْءِ الْمسْلِمِ لأَخِيهِ بظَهْرِ الغَيْبِ مُسْتَجَابَةٌ، عِنْدَ رَأْسِهِ مَلَكٌ مُوَكَّلٌ كُلَّما دَعَا لأَخِيهِ بخَيْرٍ، قالَ المَلَكُ الموَكَّلُ بهِ، آمِينَ وَلَكَ بمِثْلٍ
>
> *"The supplication of a Muslim for his [Muslim] brother in his absence will certainly be answered. Every time he makes a supplication for good for his brother, the Angel appointed for this particular task says, 'Amīn! May it be for you, too.'"*[219]

The Prophet ﷺ also said:

> الْمُؤْمِنُ لِلْمُؤْمِنِ كَالْبُنْيَانِ، يَشُدُّ بَعْضُهُ بَعْضًا، وَشَبَّكَ بَيْنَ أَصَابِعِهِ
>
> *"The relationship of the Mu'min with another Mu'min is like [the bricks of] a building; each strengthens the other." He illustrated this by interlacing the fingers of both his hands.*[220]

From the seven whom Allāh will shade on the Day of Resurrection are two who love each other for the sake of Allāh and separate for His sake. If you are reading this, take a moment to ask what it *really* means to love for Allāh's sake? By Allāh's will, we will expound on this further in the forthcoming section.

Merciful Brotherhood Even Enters Islām's Penal Code

In the age of Human Rights, antagonists of Islām have focused their criticisms on Islām's penal code, presuming that it is its Achilles heel. What is conveniently overlooked is that, under an Islāmic system, penal punishments are not meted out on

---

[218] Abu al-Dardā' says *'kāna yaqūl'* (he would say)

[219] *Ṣaḥīḥ* Muslim on the authority of Abu al-Dardā' (raḍiy Allāhu ʿanhu)

[220] *Ṣaḥīḥ* Bukhārī and Muslim on the authority of Abu Mūsā (raḍiy Allāhu ʿanhu)

mere fellow humans who deserve rights, but on your *siblings* and all that that entails. Can the same be said about any other system in the world?

Even in cases of capital punishment for murder, Allāh appeals to Ukhuwwah to calm emotions of the victim's family and to encourage amnesty. Recall that in cases of murder, the authority to punish or forgive often lies squarely with the victim's family. Read the following, which is one of many abundant examples in the Qur'ān:

> يَا أَيُّهَا الَّذِينَ آمَنُوا كُتِبَ عَلَيْكُمُ الْقِصَاصُ فِي الْقَتْلَى ۖ الْحُرُّ بِالْحُرِّ وَالْعَبْدُ بِالْعَبْدِ وَالْأُنثَىٰ بِالْأُنثَىٰ ۚ
> فَمَنْ عُفِيَ لَهُ مِنْ أَخِيهِ شَيْءٌ فَاتِّبَاعٌ بِالْمَعْرُوفِ وَأَدَاءٌ إِلَيْهِ بِإِحْسَانٍ
>
> *You who have Īmān! Retaliation is prescribed for you in the case of people killed: free man for free man, slave for slave, female for female. But if someone is absolved* ***by his brother*** *(pardoned from retaliation), blood money should be claimed with correctness and paid with good will.*[221]

In the most touching reminder of Allāh's mercy in an otherwise legal verse, the killer of *your* relative is referred to not as a murderer, assailant, or enemy, but as *your brother*.[222] Who dares claim, after this, that Islām actively seeks to punish or chastise? May Allāh give us strength and understanding.

[221] Al-Qur'ān 2:178
[222] *Tafsīr al-Ḥujurāt* – Muḥammad Metwalī al-Shaʿrāwī

THE BELIEVERS ARE NOTHING BUT *BROTHERS*

Ukhuwwah is one of the founding pillars of Islām in society. It is the second of Islām's two main objectives, coming after the Tawḥīd of Allāh. Perhaps the first of the noble Prophet's ﷺ endeavours ahead of establishing the first Muslim state in Madīnah was to form impeccable relationships between Muslims and Allāh and between Muslims and one another. Remember the context of *al-Ḥujurāt*. Such is the cornerstone of coherent groups, societies, institutions, projects and states:

> إِنَّمَا الْمُؤْمِنُونَ إِخْوَةٌ فَأَصْلِحُوا بَيْنَ أَخَوَيْكُمْ ۚ وَاتَّقُوا اللَّهَ لَعَلَّكُمْ تُرْحَمُونَ
>
> *The Mu'minūn are brothers, so make peace between your brothers and have Taqwā of Allāh so that hopefully you will gain mercy.*[223]

It is due to one's relationship with Allāh that Islāmic brotherhood manages to transcend blood relationships. While the latter links siblings biologically by way of a common mother, father, or both, the first links creatures by way of servitude to their Creator. Allāh says:

> لَّا تَجِدُ قَوْمًا يُؤْمِنُونَ بِاللَّهِ وَالْيَوْمِ الْآخِرِ يُوَادُّونَ مَنْ حَادَّ اللَّهَ وَرَسُولَهُ وَلَوْ كَانُوا آبَاءَهُمْ أَوْ أَبْنَاءَهُمْ أَوْ إِخْوَانَهُمْ أَوْ عَشِيرَتَهُمْ...
>
> *You will not find people who have Īmān in Allāh and the Last Day having love for anyone who opposes Allāh and His Messenger, though they be their fathers, their sons, their brothers or their clan...*[224]

Through this, the Prophet's companions achieved the near impossible after a 120-year-old pre-Islāmic era of sworn hostility. They would later send armies westwards to Rome, eastwards into Persia and into the depths of Africa and Asia. Anything lesser than the purpose their brotherhood was established could not break it, even with the wealth of the entire world. Such a relationship, by inverse implication, could not have been developed by the wealth of the entire world:

[223] Al-Qur'ān 49:10
[224] Al-Qur'ān 58:22

> وَأَلَّفَ بَيْنَ قُلُوبِهِمْ ۚ لَوْ أَنفَقْتَ مَا فِي الْأَرْضِ جَمِيعًا مَّا أَلَّفْتَ بَيْنَ قُلُوبِهِمْ وَلَٰكِنَّ اللَّهَ أَلَّفَ بَيْنَهُمْ ۚ إِنَّهُ عَزِيزٌ حَكِيمٌ
>
> *And [Allāh] unified their hearts. Even if you had spent everything on the Earth, you could not have unified their hearts. But Allāh has unified them. He is Almighty, All-Wise.*[225]

Everything material upon which other relationships are established became contentedly dispensable. They saw through their tribes, social statuses and wealth, and collectively aimed to serve Allāh and His religion. They rushed to obey their guide, the Messenger ﷺ, and excelled together.

How Can We Actualise 'Ukhuwwah'?

How do we begin feeling like siblings in Īmān? To wish good for one another is the very beginning. If others have been blessed with what you desire, you have been blessed with what they desire. If they have reached success through hard work, either that opportunity is also available to you, or you are excused from even pursuing it. If they are famous, then know that with fame comes burden and superficiality. If you feel obscure, then with obscurity comes inner peace and authenticity. If they have reached the stars, accompany them to the moon. Sometimes accompanying great people takes you even higher than competing with them.

If you wish anything less for them than you do for yourself, ask yourself, are they not the slaves of Allāh? Do they not yearn for the destination you yearn for and fear Hell as you do? Do they not pray in the same direction as you and face your Lord? Are they not passengers on a ship you also sail on? What benefit does their detriment bring to you and what detriment does their benefit bring to you? The Prophet ﷺ tells us:

> لَا يُؤْمِنُ أَحَدُكُمْ، حَتَّى يُحِبَّ لِأَخِيهِ مَا يُحِبُّ لِنَفْسِهِ
>
> *"No one of you has Īmān until he loves for his brother what he loves for himself."*[226]

[225] Al-Qur'ān 8:63
[226] *Ṣaḥīḥ* Bukhārī and Muslim Anas b. Mālik (raḍiy Allāhu ʿanhu)

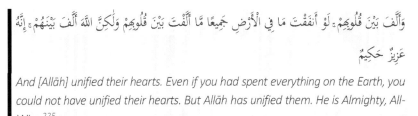

Seek out means to join the hearts, not to drive them apart. Search relentlessly for excuses, work on terms of agreement, and overlook one another's mistakes. If we are told to abandon an action that is recommended and rewardable if it causes upset, it stands to reason that such should be our attitude for all that is less than recommended too. Is that space a brother has 'reserved' on the front row worth a fight just because prayer spaces cannot technically be reserved? Is the purpose of Ṣalāh to declare a toe-to-toe war and are you really teaching the Sunnah or making a point carried by your irritation? Ibn Taymiyyah said:

> *"It is recommended (Mustahab) to leave a recommended action for the sake of bringing hearts together... the benefit of bringing together the hearts in Dīn is greater than that brought about through doing such things."*[227]

Bitterness triggers pettiness. We find that we are able to overlook our child slamming the door or their temper tantrums, but we burn and rage if we are not handed a wedding invite or if our Salām is mistakenly ignored. Pettiness holds back big ideas and cripples otherwise strong societies and teams. It creates lingering thoughts and fills your mind with pseudo-debates. If nothing else, bitterness puts unnecessary weight on the heart that is otherwise a vessel for Īmān. Maybe through this lens we can better understand how Īmān is better accommodated in a serene, cordial heart. As the Prophet ﷺ said:

> لاَ تَدْخُلُونَ الْجَنَّةَ حَتَّى تُؤْمِنُوا وَلاَ تُؤْمِنُوا حَتَّى تَحَابُّوا . أَوَلاَ أَدُلُّكُمْ عَلَى شَىْءٍ إِذَا فَعَلْتُمُوهُ تَحَابَبْتُمْ أَفْشُوا السَّلاَمَ بَيْنَكُمْ
>
> *"You will not enter Paradise until you have Īmān, and you will not have Īmān until you love one another. Shall I not tell you of that which will strengthen love between you? Spread [the greeting of] salām (peace) amongst yourselves."*[228]

He also said:

---

[227] *Majmū' al-Fatāwā* (22/407) – Ibn Taymiyyah

[228] *Ṣaḥīḥ* Muslim on the authority of Abu Hurairah (raḍiy Allāhu 'anhu)

> تَرَى الْمُؤْمِنِينَ فِي تَرَاحُمِهِمْ وَتَوَادِّهِمْ وَتَعَاطُفِهِمْ كَمَثَلِ الْجَسَدِ إِذَا اشْتَكَى عُضْوًا تَدَاعَى لَهُ سَائِرُ جَسَدِهِ بِالسَّهَرِ وَالْحُمَّى
>
> *"You see the Mu'minīn as regards their being merciful among themselves and showing love among themselves and being kind, resembling one body, so that, if any part of the body is not well, the whole body shares the insomnia and fever with it."*[229]

When exposed to trauma, the body instinctively determines which limb to sacrifice. If you fall, or you see something coming your way, your hands will fling in front of your eyes in defence. If you are left to choose between saving *any* limb and your eyes, you instinctively choose your eyes, our two 'beloved limbs'. Your eyes, however, will not find sleep if your hands were hurt defending them! The ummah is not only as connected as a body but as interdependent as one. True brotherhood is as elucidated in the couplets attributed to ʿAlī (raḍiy Allāhu ʿanhu):

إن أخاك الصدق من كان معك ومن يضر نفسه لينفعك

ومن إذا ريب الزمان صدعك شتت فيك شمله ليجمعك

"Your true friend is the one who is with you, harming himself to benefit you. The one who, if the misfortune of time shatters you, will disband himself to gather you."

The Prophet ﷺ said:

> الْمُسْلِمُ أَخُو الْمُسْلِمِ، لَا يَظْلِمُهُ، وَلَا يَخْذُلُهُ، وَلَا يَحْقِرُهُ، التَّقْوَى هَا هُنَا، وَيُشِيرُ إِلَى صَدْرِهِ ثَلَاثَ مِرَارٍ، بِحَسْبِ امْرِئٍ مِنَ الشَّرِّ أَنْ يَحْقِرَ أَخَاهُ الْمُسْلِمَ...
>
> *"The Muslim is the brother of another Muslim. He does not oppress him, nor does he disgrace him, nor does he hold him in contempt. Taqwā is here (pointing to his chest three times). It is evil enough for a person to hold his Muslim brother in contempt..."*[230]

---

[229] *Ṣaḥīḥ* Bukhārī on the authority of An-Nuʿmān b. Bashīr (raḍiy Allāhu ʿanhu)
[230] *Ṣaḥīḥ* Muslim on the authority of Abu Hurairah (raḍiy Allāhu ʿanhu)

'He does not oppress him.' Oppression is not only between the leader and the led, but between you and all whom you encounter. It is a person's divinely authorised right that his Salām is answered and his invitation is accepted. If this is the case when you are the recipient of a virtue your sibling in Īmān initiated, what then of their sanctity when taking their wealth, slandering them, tarnishing their reputation through 'exposés' or the like for a few vain likes and shares? In another narration in Bukhārī and Muslim, the Prophet ﷺ says, *'walā yuslimuh'*, meaning that *'he does not hand him over'* to his own evil, or to anything or anyone who will bring about his harm.

'He does not hold him in contempt.' The sensation of superiority is often lent to the material; more money, a bigger house, a faster car or a better paying job. But maybe more serious is that sensation entering the circles of some who feel that they have a monopoly on the Sunnah, Tawḥīd, and salvation, whilst others are considered small, worthless, and impermissible to 'sit with', defaming them as innovators who are destined to Hell. The Prophet ﷺ tells us, *"pride means denying the truth and looking down on people,"* an atom's weight of which is enough to shield one from entering Paradise.[231] Why? Because *"Taqwā is here [in the heart]."*

Taqwā is Inextricably Linked to Ukhuwwah

In reviewing the Qur'ān and Sunnah, one will very often find brotherhood mentioned alongside Taqwā. The above ḥadīth mentions *'Taqwā is here [in the heart]'* just a few sentences after *'the Muslim is the brother of another Muslim.'* In the verse of *al-Ḥujurāt*, Allāh says:

> *The Mu'minūn are brothers... and have Taqwā of Allāh.*[232]

Later, within this context, Allāh tells us:

> *The noblest among you in Allah's sight is the one with the most Taqwā...*[233]

Elsewhere in the Qur'ān, He says:

---

[231] *Ṣaḥīḥ* Bukhārī and Muslim on the authority of ʿAbdullāh b. ʿUmar (raḍiy Allāhu ʿanhu)
[232] Al-Qur'ān 49:10
[233] Al-Qur'ān 49:13

> يَا أَيُّهَا الَّذِينَ آمَنُوا اتَّقُوا اللَّهَ حَقَّ تُقَاتِهِ وَلَا تَمُوتُنَّ إِلَّا وَأَنتُم مُّسْلِمُونَ ۞ وَاعْتَصِمُوا بِحَبْلِ اللَّهِ جَمِيعًا وَلَا تَفَرَّقُوا ۚ وَاذْكُرُوا نِعْمَتَ اللَّهِ عَلَيْكُمْ إِذْ كُنتُمْ أَعْدَاءً فَأَلَّفَ بَيْنَ قُلُوبِكُمْ فَأَصْبَحْتُم بِنِعْمَتِهِ إِخْوَانًا وَكُنتُمْ عَلَىٰ شَفَا حُفْرَةٍ مِّنَ النَّارِ فَأَنقَذَكُم مِّنْهَا ۗ ...
>
> *You who have Īmān, have **Taqwā of Allāh** as is His due and do not die except as Muslims. And remember Allāh's Favour on you, for you were enemies one to another but He joined your hearts together, so that, by His Grace, **you became brethren** [in Islāmic faith], and you were on the brink of a pit of Fire, and He saved you from it...*[234]

In another verse, He informs us:

> الْأَخِلَّاءُ يَوْمَئِذٍ بَعْضُهُمْ لِبَعْضٍ عَدُوٌّ إِلَّا الْمُتَّقِينَ
>
> ***Close friends**, that Day, will be enemies to each other, except for the **Muttaqīn**.*[235]

Without doubt, Taqwā is inextricably linked to Ukhuwwah, and yet Taqwā, or the determination of a person's real value, is hidden or divinely classified 'in the heart'. This is real food for thought. People are oppressed, disgraced, or held in contempt because of their being perceived as inferior. But since the criterion upon which the culprit created his 'superior' perception is hidden, there is *nothing* material upon which to definitely conclude one's superiority over another! And in Islām, the main criterion for real nobility is Taqwā, or observance or consciousness of Allāh. How then can we hold any Muslim in contempt or afford them anything less than honour and respect when we have no idea what the Taqwā they possess looks like?

Shift your paradigm to this real benchmark. If you stand in the night in Qiyām, do not belittle those who sleep. If you fast throughout the year, do not belittle those who do not. Qiyām and fasting are virtuous, but tell yourself, what if they regret their actions, or inaction in this case, whilst I admire mine? What if they feel guilty of their sins or feel humiliated before Allāh, whilst I am impressed by my deeds? Aḥmad b. Atā Allāh al-Iskandarī said:

> رُبَّ معصية أورثت ذلاً و إنكساراً خيرٌ من طاعة أورثت عزاً و إستكباراً

[234] Al-Qur'ān 3:102-103
[235] Al-Qur'ān 43:67

> *"It may be that a sin that creates humility and a feeling of destitution to Allāh is better than an act of obedience that creates pride and arrogance."*

The events at Badr, Uḥud, al-Aḥzāb, and the conquest of Makkah leave us in awe – and rightly so. But how often do we study these feats through the lens of brotherhood? The Prophet's project of uniting hearts ahead of these mighty challenges was meticulously timed. Likewise, in the West, it is not the size of the challenges that defeat us, but our thinking that 'uniting hearts' comes after trying to address those challenges, when it is in fact the single most important goal worth pursuing after our relationship with Allāh. *'Make peace between your brothers'* because we, as a community, are much stronger as *one*. If *al-Ḥujurāt* is about fortifying the Muslim community with ethics to prepare it for world reformation, the core of *al-Ḥujurāt* is about fortifying Ukhuwwah. Allāh tells us:

> وَأَطِيعُوا اللَّهَ وَرَسُولَهُ وَلَا تَنَازَعُوا فَتَفْشَلُوا وَتَذْهَبَ رِيحُكُمْ وَاصْبِرُوا إِنَّ اللَّهَ مَعَ الصَّابِرِينَ
>
> *Obey Allāh and His Messenger and do not quarrel among yourselves lest you lose heart and your momentum disappears. And be steadfast. Allāh is with the steadfast.*[236]

Who Quarrelled in the Prophetic Community?

ʿAbdullāh b. Ubayy was the leader of the hypocrites who, in the early part of the Sīrah, was one of the leaders of the al-Khazraj clan in Madīnah. It was said that before the arrival of the Prophet ﷺ, he was a contender for the leadership of Yathrib (which later became Madīnah) after a pact between the 'Aws and the Khazraj. Anas (raḍiy Allāhu ʿanhu) narrates that he said, *"Messenger of Allāh, why not go to ʿAbdullāh b. Ubayy?"* Anas seemingly wanted the Prophet ﷺ to guide him as his devotion to Islām would have had a huge influence on his clan.

The Prophet indeed rode his mule and went to ʿAbdullāh b. Ubayy and the Muslims followed along muddy terrain. As they passed, the despicable hypocrite could not but express his animosity towards the Messenger of Allāh ﷺ, who had transformed Madīnah and gathered its tribes and clans around him. ʿAbdullāh b. Ubayy said, *"Get away from me, for by Allāh I have been disturbed by the smell of your mule."* According to some narrations, a man from the Anṣār, namely ʿAbdullāh b. Rawāha (raḍiy Allāhu

[236] Al-Qur'ān 8:46

ʿanhu), replied, *"The donkey of the Messenger of Allāh smells better than you!"* A man from ʿAbdullāh b. Ubayy's friends became infuriated and each companion became involved to defend his friend. Eventually, a fight broke out and the Muslims began exchanging blows with palm stalks, fists, and shoes. Anas said that the verse, *'If two parties of believers fight, make peace between them'* was revealed specifically about this incident.

Ibn ʿĀshūr disputes this as the reason for revelation, arguing that this particular event involving ʿAbdullāh b. Ubayy occurred in the earliest days of Madīnah, whilst *al-Ḥujurāt* was revealed in the ninth year. He says that Anas said *"**it reached us** that the verse was revealed"* without asserting with certainty that this was the case. This is unless, of course, the verse became part of this *Sūrah* many years later.[237]

It was also reported by Qatādah and al-Sudī that the verse was actually revealed about a dispute that broke out between a man and his wife, one of whom was from the tribe of Aws and the other from al-Khazraj, with each invoking their tribes for support, which ended up in a group fist-fight.

In both incidents, the Prophet ﷺ rushed to make peace between the two parties and thus this verse became a general ruling concerning a specific incident as is generally the case with reasons for revelation. Even if either incident is exactly the reason for why this verse was revealed, it does not mean that it can only be applied in an identical situation. And Allāh knows best.

---

[237] Both narrations are mentioned in a number of *Tafsīr* books. The latter discussion on what is more likely the case is mentioned in *Tafsīr al-Taḥrīr wa al-Tanwīr* – Ibn ʿĀshūr

SECTION 4: A GENERAL COLLECTION OF MANNERS AND ETHICS

A*l-Ḥujurāt* follows a natural progression of events, furnishing the Qur'ānic community with guidance in each of its verses. Those in conflict due to unverified news are entitled to their siblings in Īmān coming to their rescue, seeking the restoration of peace and the merciful ties of brotherhood. It reminds us of the reality of this unrivalled social union. The previous section concluded with Allāh showing His mercy towards those who show mercy to fellow Mu'minūn by kindling that firm sense of Ukhuwwah within them. More than outer peace through the cessation of physical hostilities, the true sense of brotherhood can only be achieved through embodying Allāh's Taqwā and dispelling those inner actions that prevent or diminish it.

It is therefore appropriate that this section outlines those actions that create malice and bitterness – both those done in the presence of your siblings and in their absence. Beyond conflicting groups, the verses in this section extend etiquettes to each and every individual within the society.

> يَا أَيُّهَا الَّذِينَ آمَنُوا لَا يَسْخَرْ قَوْمٌ مِّن قَوْمٍ عَسَىٰ أَن يَكُونُوا خَيْرًا مِّنْهُمْ وَلَا نِسَاءٌ مِّن نِّسَاءٍ عَسَىٰ
> أَن يَكُنَّ خَيْرًا مِّنْهُنَّ ۖ وَلَا تَلْمِزُوا أَنفُسَكُمْ وَلَا تَنَابَزُوا بِالْأَلْقَابِ ۖ بِئْسَ الِاسْمُ الْفُسُوقُ بَعْدَ
> الْإِيمَانِ ۚ وَمَن لَّمْ يَتُبْ فَأُولَٰئِكَ هُمُ الظَّالِمُونَ ◇ يَا أَيُّهَا الَّذِينَ آمَنُوا اجْتَنِبُوا كَثِيرًا مِّنَ الظَّنِّ إِنَّ بَعْضَ
> الظَّنِّ إِثْمٌ ۖ وَلَا تَجَسَّسُوا وَلَا يَغْتَب بَّعْضُكُم بَعْضًا ۚ أَيُحِبُّ أَحَدُكُمْ أَن يَأْكُلَ لَحْمَ أَخِيهِ مَيْتًا

> فَكَرِهْتُمُوهُ ۚ وَاتَّقُوا اللَّهَ ۚ إِنَّ اللَّهَ تَوَّابٌ رَّحِيمٌ ۞ يَا أَيُّهَا النَّاسُ إِنَّا خَلَقْنَاكُم مِّن ذَكَرٍ وَأُنثَىٰ وَجَعَلْنَاكُمْ
> شُعُوبًا وَقَبَائِلَ لِتَعَارَفُوا ۚ إِنَّ أَكْرَمَكُمْ عِندَ اللَّهِ أَتْقَاكُمْ ۚ إِنَّ اللَّهَ عَلِيمٌ خَبِيرٌ
>
> *You who have Īmān! People should not ridicule others who may be better than themselves; nor should any women ridicule other women who may be better than themselves. And do not find fault with one another or insult each other with derogatory nicknames. How evil it is to have a name for evil conduct after coming to Īmān! Those people who do not turn from it are wrongdoers. You who have Īmān! Avoid most suspicion. Indeed some suspicion is a crime. And do not spy and do not backbite one another. Would any of you like to eat his brother's dead flesh? No, you would hate it. And have Taqwā of Allāh. Allāh is Ever-Returning, Most Merciful. Mankind! We created you from a male and female, and made you into peoples and tribes so that you might come to know each other. The noblest among you in Allāh's sight is the one with the most Taqwā. Allāh is All-Knowing, All-Aware.*[238]

Verse 11

> يا أَيُّهَا الَّذينَ آمَنوا لا يَسخَر قَومٌ مِن قَومٍ عَسىٰ أَن يَكونوا خَيرًا مِنهُم وَلا نِساءٌ مِن نِساءٍ عَسىٰ
> أَن يَكُنَّ خَيرًا مِنهُنَّ ۖ وَلا تَلمِزوا أَنفُسَكُم وَلا تَنابَزوا بِالأَلقابِ ۖ بِئسَ الِاسمُ الفُسوقُ بَعدَ الإيمانِ ۚ
> وَمَن لَم يَتُب فَأُولٰئِكَ هُمُ الظّالِمون
>
> *You who have Īmān! People should not ridicule others who may be better than themselves; nor should any women ridicule other women who may be better than themselves. And do not find fault with one another or insult each other with derogatory nicknames. How evil it is to have a name for evil conduct after coming to Īmān! Those people who do not turn from it are wrongdoers.*[239]

You who have Īmān in Allāh and His Messenger, a Mu'min group must not ridicule another, because it may be that those ridiculed are better than those who are ridiculing. Likewise, a group of women must not ridicule another because it may be

---

[238] Al-Qur'ān 49:11-13
[239] Al-Qur'ān 49:11

that those ridiculed are better than those who are ridiculing. Some have reasoned that this is a specific stipulation concerning the rich ridiculing the poor for their poverty. Others have said that it specifically addresses those whose sins have been veiled mocking at those whose sins have been exposed. Such implies that every man is sinful and never escapes one of those two realities. According to Ibn Zaid:

> *"It may be that a person **exposed for his sin** is better than a person **whose sin has been hidden** ... [after all] how do you know your hidden sin will be forgiven?"*

Besides the specific example, the prohibition is general and encompasses any and every type of mockery directed at a believer.[240]

The indefinite form of 'people' (*Qawm*) is not only used to indicate how widespread ridiculing was and remains to be, but to encompass every nation or people, regardless of social status, privilege or supposed superiority. Linguistically, '*Qawm*' points to a group of men. The repeated prohibition towards women (*Nisā'*) is then to leave no segment of society unaddressed in a direct sense, lest women mistakenly think the address is exclusively directed at men.

According to others, '*Qawm*' can also linguistically encompass women.[241] In this latter case, the emphatic specification of '*Nisā'*' can then be seen to address the fact that ridicule and gossip is especially rampant in female social circles. Research in gender-specific social behaviours proves this is 'more than just anecdotal' and, instead, owes to the nature of women being *obsessed* with news about other women.[242] This does not imply women are more aggressive than men, but are different in how they dispense that aggression – through words rather than action. Other social realities are more rampant in men, such as theft, such that Allāh will admonish men more than women on those occasions!

'*[It may be that] those ridiculed are better than those who are ridiculing*' is not only for emphasis, but to express what is commonplace: that those being ridiculed are better than the perpetrators. This part of the verse should thus evoke a sense of shyness in the heart of the one ridiculing. It is not a dispensation to ridicule if one is sure that their victim is worse than him or her.[243] Usually, it is only those whose hearts are full of faults, pettiness, and genuine inferiority who find it pertinent to ridicule others.[244] It has been authentically reported that the Messenger ﷺ said:

---

[240] *Jāmiʿ al-Bayān fī Ta'wīl al-Qur'ān* – Imām al-Ṭabarī
[241] *Tafsīr al-Taḥrīr* wa al-Tanwīr – Ibn ʿĀshūr
[242] See the following (accessed March 2020):
https://www.psychologytoday.com/gb/blog/out-the-ooze/201506/is-the-tongue-the-sword-woman
[243] *Tafsīr al-Taḥrīr wa al-Tanwīr* – Ibn ʿĀshūr
[244] *Taysīr al-Karīm al-Raḥmān fī Tafsīr Kalām al-Mannān* – ʿAbdur-Raḥmān Al-Saʿdī

> الكِبْر بَطَرُ الحَقِّ وَغَمْطُ النَّاسِ
>
> *"Pride (al-Kibr) is to disdain the truth [out of self-conceit] and to hold contempt for the people."*

Ridiculing is a consequence of pride or conceit (*al-Kibr*) which is to look down on others. *'And do not find fault with one another* (*anfusakum*)*'*, meaning, do not malign or defame one another. The word *'anfusakum'* can refer both to *'one another'* and *'yourselves'*. Do not malign *yourselves* delivers the meaning that maligning and defaming your siblings in Īmān is tantamount to defaming your very self. This is because the Mu'minūn are siblings, as set out in the previous verse and are thus of a single self (*Nafs*).

In another verse, Allāh says:

> وَيْلٌ لِكُلِّ هُمَزَةٍ لُمَزَةٍ
>
> *Woe to every scorner and mocker.*[245]

The *'Hammāz'* is the one who maligns by way of action, and the *'Lammāz'* (as appears in the verse of *al-Ḥujurāt – 'talmizū'*) is the one who does so with the tongue. Both are quick in finding fault and, as such, are belittled in the eyes of others.[246] *'Al-Lamz'* is to mention someone's flaws directly to their face. If it happens that such flaws actually exist in the victim, then such an action remains to be shameless and belligerent, and if they do not, then it is shameless and slanderous.[247]

What is interpreted as *'and do not insult each other with derogatory nicknames'* contain terms from *'al-Nabz'* and *'al-Laqab'*. Both are similar in meaning and the verse can be understood to mean, *'do not label others with labels.'* More specifically, the prohibition covers those names that people hate to be called. This includes calling the Muslim a deviator (*Fāsiq*), a fornicator (*Zāni*), a hypocrite (*Munāfiq*), a disbeliever (*Kāfir*) and the like. It furthermore includes names that serve to remind a person of their sins before embracing Islām or before desisting and repenting. The lack of specificity in the verse goes to encompass every label or characteristic disliked by its recipient.[248]

'How evil it is to have a name for evil conduct (*Fusūq*) *after coming to Īmān'*. The Arabic text of the verse can be understood as: If you insist on giving one another

---

[245] Al-Qur'ān 104:1

[246] *Tafsīr al-Qur'ān al-'Aẓīm* – Ibn Kathīr

[247] *Tafsīr al-Taḥrīr wa al-Tanwīr* – Ibn 'Āshūr

[248] *Jāmi' al-Bayān fī Ta'wīl al-Qur'ān* – Imām al-Ṭabarī

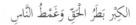

derogatory labels, sinning against Allāh after your Īmān and ridiculing those of Īmān, then such a labeller earns the label of *Fāsiq*. Others have said, as is the chosen meaning in the translation, that Allāh is declaring the evilness of labelling a Muslim with the label of *Fusūq*. Both meanings can be carried by the verse, but al-Ṭabarī favours the first and sees it more fitting with the context of admonition.[249] That admonition is, moreover, suited to the original offence such that throwing accusations of *Fusūq* ends up rebounding back to the source, as in the aforementioned maxim: you reap what you sow.

'Those people who do not turn from it are wrongdoers', meaning that those who do not repent from labelling, defaming, or ridiculing their siblings in Īmān have wronged themselves and become deserving of Allāh's punishment.[250] How then does such a person become a *'Ẓālim'* (*an oppressor*)? Besides oppressing his victims, such a person oppresses his own self by wilfully exposing it to punishment in the Hereafter despite being very able to desist from those vices. With the severity of Hell in mind, the latter oppression overwhelms the former. The wording of the verse also stresses that the culprit is almost exclusively the victim of their own assault. Read it again:

'Those [the culprits] are (*ulā'ika*), *themselves* (*hum*) the oppressors *Ẓālimūn*.'[251]

Ridiculing your Sibling is Never Justified

One is never in a position to ridicule. If the deficiency exists in the victim's religion or manners, it becomes incumbent on the one who identifies this deficiency to rectify it. If it is of a physical nature, then one should show respect towards the One who created the victim as such, recognising one's own plentiful physical deficiencies. Ridicule, as mentioned, only stems from those who deem themselves superior over their victim in one observable aspect or another. Had the culprit taken a moment to think, they would see the victim superseding them in many other aspects. People's abilities may be specifically unequal but ultimately equal. This divine will is to facilitate society's function and to promote togetherness and cooperation. Those who excel in certain spheres provide service to those who need them. Allāh says in another verse:

وَرَفَعنا بَعضَهُم فَوقَ بَعضٍ دَرَجاتٍ لِيَتَّخِذَ بَعضُهُم بَعضًا سُخرِيًّا...

[249] *Jāmiʿ al-Bayān fī Ta'wīl al-Qur'ān* – Imām al-Ṭabarī

[250] *Jāmiʿ al-Bayān fī Ta'wīl al-Qur'ān* – Imām al-Ṭabarī

[251] *Tafsīr al-Taḥrīr wa al-Tanwīr* – Ibn ʿĀshūr

> *We have allocated their livelihood among them in the life of the Dunya and raised some of them above others in rank* ***that they may make use of one another for service...***[252]

There must exist those who are above in aspects over those below. If a prince were to find that the palace's sewage system was broken, he would rush to hire a plumber to address the appalling smell. In such an example, the prince is above the plumber in the sphere of wealth, but the plumber is above the prince in his vital ability to fix drains! The prince cannot function without a plumber, and the plumber cannot function without an income. By recognising people's interdependency and ultimate equality if all of their abilities are assessed collectively, the natural conclusion is that ridicule is always unfounded.[253] May Allāh guide us to the best manners and ethics. And all strength is from Allāh.

---

[252] Al-Qur'ān 43:32

[253] *Tafsīr al-Ḥujurāt* – Muḥammad Metwalī al-Shaʿrāwī

SUSPICION, SPYING AND BACKBITING – A NATURAL PROGRESSION

In the previous section we explored how *al-Ḥujurāt* addresses a collection of interpersonal social ills including ridicule, fault-finding, insult, and name-calling. Unlike the Qur'ān, man-inspired legislation only goes as far as to deal with conscious manifestations of evil conduct. *Al-Ḥujurāt* vividly demonstrates the transcendence of Islām's social code. It deals with the secret and private, including the evils of the heart and mind. Although some will dub this as controlling, such regulation exists to weed out the causes of conflict and disunity before they have a chance to materialise into the physical realm.

Verse 12

> يا أَيُّهَا الَّذينَ آمَنوا اجتَنِبوا كَثيرًا مِنَ الظَّنِّ إِنَّ بَعضَ الظَّنِّ إِثمٌ ۖ وَلا تَجَسَّسوا وَلا يَغتَب بَعضُكُم
> بَعضًا ۚ أَيُحِبُّ أَحَدُكُم أَن يَأكُلَ لَحمَ أَخيهِ مَيتًا فَكَرِهتُموهُ ۚ وَاتَّقُوا اللَّهَ ۚ إِنَّ اللَّهَ تَوّابٌ رَحيمٌ
>
> *You who have Īmān, avoid most suspicion. Indeed, some suspicion is a crime. And do not spy and do not backbite one another. Would any of you like to eat his brother's dead flesh? No, you would hate it. And have Taqwā of Allāh. Allāh is Ever-Returning, Most Merciful.*[254]

Immediately after exhorting those of Īmān to not call one another derogatory names, Allāh, the Most Merciful addresses us again with a final and intense appeal to our most eminent name, '*You who have Īmān*'. He is thus the first to implement that highest legislation, honouring, rather than disparaging us. The appeal to Īmān is again used for the sake of distinction and importance, urging us to adopt those covert and internal actions and ethics due of a Mu'min. It begins with an address to those who have Īmān in Allāh and His Messenger ﷺ to not come near to '*a lot of suspicion*', for much of it is evil. 'A lot' is not to forbid suspicion entirely, because in other instances, Allāh encourages us to suspect good of one another, like when He says:[255]

---

[254] Al-Qur'ān 49:12

[255] *Jāmi' al-Bayān fī Ta'wīl al-Qur'ān* – Imām al-Ṭabarī

> لَّوْلَا إِذْ سَمِعْتُمُوهُ ظَنَّ الْمُؤْمِنُونَ وَالْمُؤْمِنَاتُ بِأَنفُسِهِمْ خَيْرًا وَقَالُوا هَٰذَا إِفْكٌ مُّبِينٌ
>
> *Why, when you heard it, did you not, as men and women of the Mu'minūn, instinctively think good thoughts and say, 'This is obviously a lie'?*[256]

Other types of suspicion may even be necessary, such as in times of war. The Mu'minūn are encouraged to utter their good suspicion, even if unsure of its veracity, but should not harbour evil suspicion, let alone utter it. As such, the Mu'min is given the privilege of being thought good of. Avoiding *'a lot of suspicion'* is thus to err on the side of caution, just in case it leads one into evil suspicion. ʿUmar (raḍiy Allāhu ʿanhu) is reported to have said:

> *"Only suspect good of any word uttered by your brother, if it is remotely possible to interpret it to have meant good."*[257]

The Prophet ﷺ said:

> إِيَّاكُمْ وَالظَّنَّ، فَإِنَّ الظَّنَّ أَكْذَبُ الْحَدِيثِ
>
> *"Beware of suspicion because suspicion is the most untrue of all speech."*[258]

Evil forms of suspicion may naturally occur in the mind and escape one's control. Such is not what is intended here, but one must exert an effort to challenge even fleeting evil suspicion. If you are unable to establish the veracity of suspicious thought, *belie yourself* and struggle against it until you manage to overcome it.[259]

'And do not spy'. Do not actively investigate one another's secrets in pursuit of finding one other's faults. Reason with what is immediately apparent (*Ẓāhir*) to you and praise or censure according to this and not by what you discover.[260] *Tajassus* is not restricted to looking through a keyhole, as per the typical image of spying, but is to scrounge for your sibling's flaws and to build judgements about what you have gone out of your way to find.

---

[256] Al-Qur'ān 24:12
[257] *Tafsīr al-Qur'ān al-ʿAẓīm* – Ibn Kathīr
[258] *Ṣaḥīḥ* Bukhārī and Muslim on the authority of Abu Hurairah (raḍiy Allāhu ʿanhu)
[259] *Tafsīr al-Taḥrīr wa al-Tanwīr* – Ibn ʿĀshūr
[260] *Jāmiʿ al-Bayān fī Ta'wīl al-Qur'ān* – Imām al-Ṭabarī

'And do not backbite one another'. Do not say something about another person in their absence that they would despise to be told upfront.[261] Realise that it is about what *they* would despise to be told, not what *you* would hate to tell them.[262] The Prophet ﷺ asked his companions:

> أَتَدْرُونَ مَا الْغِيبَةُ. قَالُوا اللَّهُ وَرَسُولُهُ أَعْلَمُ. قَالَ، ذِكْرُكَ أَخَاكَ بِمَا يَكْرَهُ. قِيلَ، أَفَرَأَيْتَ إِنْ كَانَ فِي أَخِي مَا أَقُولُ قَالَ، إِنْ كَانَ فِيهِ مَا تَقُولُ فَقَدِ اغْتَبْتَهُ وَإِنْ لَمْ يَكُنْ فِيهِ فَقَدْ بَهَتَّهُ
>
> *"Do you know what backbiting is?" They (the Companions) said, "Allāh and His Messenger know best." Thereupon he (the Prophet) said, "Backbiting implies your talking about your brother in a manner which he does not like." It was said to him, "What if I actually find [that failing] in my brother which I made a mention of?" He said, "If [that failing] is actually found [in him] as you state, you have in fact backbitten him, and if not, you have slandered him."*[263]

The companion ʿAbdullāh b. Mas'ūd (raḍiy Allāhu ʿanhu) says:

> *"No morsel of food is worse than backbiting your brother. 'Would any of you like to eat his brother's dead flesh? No, you would hate it.'"*

'Would one of you desire to eat his brother's dead flesh?' means after his death. Just as you would wholly despise to eat from your brother's rotting corpse – not least that it is impure and Ḥarām – you should despise speaking ill of your brother behind his back whilst alive.[264] Make equal the feeling you have towards both. The power of this Qur'ānic resemblance, metaphorically speaking, can be viewed in three ways:

- The backbiter is 'consuming the flesh' through defaming another's reputation – thereby 'eating into' or reducing their presence and honour.

- The victim is his 'brother' (or sister) in Islām.

---

[261] *Jāmiʿ al-Bayān fī Ta'wīl al-Qur'ān* – Imām al-Ṭabarī
[262] Some will say "I would tell them to their face" as if this undoes the backbiting. The question is not what you would be willing to tell them to their face, but rather, would they like to hear it being told to their face at the point you said it in their absence?
[263] Ṣaḥīḥ Muslim on the authority of Abu Hurairah (raḍiy Allāhu ʿanhu)
[264] *Jāmiʿ al-Bayān fī Ta'wīl al-Qur'ān* – Imām al-Ṭabarī

- It is as 'in a state of his [or her] death' by it being in their absence and their inability to defend themselves at the moment of that defamation, much like if they were lifeless.[265]

'And have Taqwā of Allāh' by avoiding His prohibitions including: evil suspicion, searching for your sibling's faults, exposing what Allāh has hidden, backbiting, as well as other divine prohibitions. *'Allāh is Ever-Returning, Most Merciful'*. He is ever-returning to His servant what that servant wants from his Lord, if that servant returns to his Lord what his Lord wants from His servant. And Allāh is Most-Merciful (*Raḥīm*), never punishing after repentance.[266]

Injunctions Imply their Opposite

The prohibitions outlined in these verses of *al-Ḥujurāt* should be seen as inferring the opposite etiquette.[267] In other words, to not ridicule others infers that one should speak highly of and encourage others. If ridicule demoralises, a Muslim should exhibit behaviours that boost morale. To not find fault with one another infers looking for and informing of one another's assets and competences. This also means to speak of areas in which one's siblings in Islām excel rather than where they fall short, to overlook their human flaws and find justifications for their misbehaviours.

To not insult each other with derogatory nicknames infers using honourable and inspiring titles. Recall how the Prophet ﷺ addressed his companions with hugely uplifting names. Hamzah was labelled the Lion of Allāh, Khālid the Sword of Allāh, Abu Bakr the *Ṣiddīq*, ʿUmar the *Fārūq*, Ṭalha the living martyr, ʿUthman the one from whom the Angels are shy of and al-Zubair the Prophet's *'Hawāri'* (disciple). The Prophet ﷺ said:

> إِنَّ لِكُلِّ نَبِيٍّ حَوَارِيًّا، وَإِنَّ حَوَارِيَّ الزُّبَيْرُ بْنُ الْعَوَّامِ
>
> *"Every prophet used to have a Hawāri, and my Hawāri is Al-Zubair b. Al-ʿAwwām."*[268]

One can argue that the Prophet ﷺ was simply stating truths. But even as statements of truth, imagine the effect stating them had on the companions and the encouragement and zeal they would have inspired. Now imagine if the companions

[265] *Tafsīr al-Taḥrīr wa al-Tanwīr* – Ibn ʿĀshūr
[266] *Jāmiʿ al-Bayān fī Ta'wīl al-Qur'ān* – Imām al-Ṭabarī
[267] *Tafsīr al-Taḥrīr wa al-Tanwīr* – Ibn ʿĀshūr
[268] *Ṣaḥīḥ* Bukhārī on the authority of Jābir b. ʿAbdullāh (raḍiy Allāhu ʿanhu)

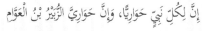

had been defined and labelled by their human mistakes, which are also truths, and how this would have diffused their passion and weakened their resolve.

To avoid most suspicion infers that a Muslim should suspect the *best* in other Muslims. Suspect in them what you would suspect of yourself. *'Do not spy'* infers that if your sibling has flawed in secret, find ways of keeping those flaws hidden. If you have learnt of their flaws after rummaging for them, continue on as if not having heard or seen anything at all. *'Do not backbite one another'* infers speaking well of those absent, particular those one has disparaged before. There is no risk of inflating egos by spreading one another's virtues in absentia!

Evil Suspicion Leads to Spying Which Leads to Backbiting

How do spying and backbiting, mentioned second and third in verse 12, relate to the evil suspicion that introduces it? Think of the following example. Person A sees person B driving a lavish car. Person B is known for being insolvent. As such, person A begins to harbour evil suspicions about person B, questioning the source of that income. If not belied and resisted, person A chooses to further investigate (i.e. spy) the private matters of B to that effect. If person A finds nothing, he may have already settled on his scepticism, proceeding to speaking ill about person B in his absence (backbiting).

Alternatively, person A will use anything he discovers to validate his suspicion or may actually discover what does, in fact, validate his suspicion. But even in this latter case, not only was his exposition of person B's sin through backbiting a sin, his covert investigation itself was a sin! Ibn ʿĀshūr mentions that harbouring and nurturing evil suspicion is bound to cause it to seem like certain knowledge. Everything one sees afterwards then validates those forged certainties.[269] Recall Banī al-Mustaliq mentioned earlier. Al-Walīd b. ʿUqbah (raḍiy Allāhu ʿanhu) suspected that the tribe would display hostility and not pay the Zakāh. When they came intending to pay the Zakāh, al-Walīd saw their assemblage and weapons as validating his suspicion because he did not question it. In cognitive science, the tendency to interpret or favour information in a way that confirms one's preconceived beliefs or hypotheses is termed Confirmation Bias.[270]

If spying (*Tajassus*) emerges from evil suspicion (*Ẓann*), then if we take it back further, *Tajassus* and *Ẓann* are two actions that ravage brotherhood (reference to which is made in the preceding verse). Spying only takes place when there exists a lack of trust and, if discovered, the victim also ceases to trust the perpetrator, maybe even

[269] *Tafsīr al-Taḥrīr wa al-Tanwīr* – Ibn ʿĀshūr

[270] Plous, Scott (1993), The Psychology of Judgment and Decision Making, p. 233

seeking revenge or triggering a fight – as addressed earlier in *al-Ḥujurāt*. Thus, we see how the messages of *al-Ḥujurāt* are meticulously sequenced and intertwined.

It is worth mentioning that although it is necessary not to harbour suspicion against other Muslims, it is also important for us not to unnecessarily draw suspicious thoughts towards ourselves. For example, if we are travelling or ill, there is no need to eat in public during Ramaḍān. If we are newly married, we should make it known that the person we are walking with is our spouse, and so on. Our mother Safiyyah (raḍiy Allāhu ʿanhā) said:

> *"I came to visit the Prophet ﷺ while he was in the state of Iʿtikāf (seclusion during the last ten days of Ramaḍān). After having talked to him, I got up to return. The Prophet ﷺ also got up with me and accompanied me a part of the way. At that moment two Anṣāri men passed by. When they saw him, they quickened their pace. The Prophet ﷺ said to them, 'Do not hurry. She is Safiyyah, daughter of Huyay, my wife.' They said: 'Subḥān Allāh O Messenger of Allāh! (meaning you are far away from any suspicion).' The Messenger of Allāh ﷺ said, 'The Shayṭān circulates in a person like blood [in the veins]. I apprehended lest the Shayṭān should drop some evil thoughts in your minds.'"*[271]

This is the Messenger of Allāh ﷺ. We are much more in need of such caution and of assisting the hearts of those around us.

Repenting from Ghībah

Even something as severe as backbiting can be forgiven, as per the end of verse 12. But true repentance is to first *stop* backbiting the victim, then to sincerely intend to not backbite them again. One should embody a sense of regret for what was said in the past. Finally, one should seek the victim's forgiveness. Oftentimes, informing the victim of their being spoken ill of will cause more upset than if the sin were to be kept hidden. In such cases, many scholars have said that instead of informing the victim, one should try to undo the sin by praising that person *in a similar setting* to the one they were censured in. Otherwise, one may also strive to protect that person from others backbiting them. Their defence will, *in shā Allāh*, serve to make up for their own initial backbiting.[272] The Prophet ﷺ said:

[271] *Ṣaḥīḥ* Bukhārī and Muslim on the authority of Safiyyah (raḍiy Allāhu ʿanhā)
[272] *Tafsīr al-Qur'ān al-ʿAẓīm* – Ibn Kathīr

> مَنْ حَمَى مُؤْمِنًا مِنْ مُنَافِقٍ بَعَثَ اللَّهُ مَلَكًا يَحْمِي لَحْمَهُ يَوْمَ الْقِيَامَةِ مِنْ نَارِ جَهَنَّمَ وَمَنْ رَمَى مُسْلِمًا بِشَيْءٍ يُرِيدُ شَيْنَهُ بِهِ حَبَسَهُ اللَّهُ عَلَى جِسْرِ جَهَنَّمَ حَتَّى يَخْرُجَ مِمَّا قَالَ
>
> *"If anyone guards a believer from a hypocrite, Allāh will send an Angel who will guard his flesh on the Day of Resurrection from the fire of Jahannam, but if anyone attacks a Muslim saying something by which he wishes to disgrace him, he will be restrained by Allāh on the bridge over Jahannam until he is acquitted of what he said."*[273]

Concealing the faults of a Mu'min is in fact one of the Divine Attributes of Allāh. Those Characteristics of Allāh that are transitive in nature (*Muta'addī*), extending to His creatures (the objects) usually have a related opposite. For instance, Allāh is the One Who gives honour (*Mu'iz*) and the One Who debases (*Mudhil*); the One Who gives life (*al-Muḥyī*) and the One the Who gives death (*al-Mumīt*); the One Who extends (*al-Bāsiṭ*) and the One Who withholds (*al-Qābiḍ*), and so on.

However, His Absolute Characteristics, those intransitive in nature (*Lāzim*) and not extending to others naturally do not have others that oppose them. The absolute name of *al-Ḥayy*, for instance, which means the Ever-Living, does not have an opposite befitting of Allāh. One of Allāh's absolute names is *al-Sittīr* (the One Who covers).[274] This means that He is the One Who absolutely covers the faults of His slaves without a befitting opposite. This emphasises how much He dislikes that the faults of His slaves are exposed. For a sinner to wish that their sin was hidden proves that he or she still possesses a glimmer of Īmān, enough to beget a sense of shyness.[275] And Allāh knows best.

---

[273] *Sunan* Abī Dāwūd on the authority of Mu'adh b. Anas (raḍiy Allāhu 'anhu)

[274] *Sunan* an-Nasā'ī on the authority of Safwan b. Ya'lā from his father Ya'lā

[275] *Tafsīr al-Ḥujurāt* – Muḥammad Metwalī al-Sha'rāwī

THE FINAL CALL TO ALL OF MANKIND

Now comes the final call, which, unlike the preceding five calls, is not only addressed to those of Īmān, but to all of humanity. It is one that sets the benchmark and criterion for true nobility until the end of time. It is at once the ultimate, divine proclamation against tribalism, nationalism, and xenophobia; ills that were rampant during the era of pre-Islāmic ignorance (*Jāhiliyyah*). It is a firm premise for unity and coexistence that comforted many of Islām's newest entrants who hailed from lower social statuses or lineages, or were slaves from unknown ancestries.

In the Qur'ān, whenever the *'Mu'minūn'* are addressed, an instruction follows. The addressee is then inspired to observe that instruction by virtue of their Īmān. Conversely, when 'people' are addressed, what usually follows are universal truths, including matters of *ʿAqīdah* and others concerning establishing Īmān in people's hearts. These universal realities naturally encompass everyone, Mu'min and Kāfir.

Verse 13

> يا أَيُّها النّاسُ إِنّا خَلَقناكُم مِن ذَكَرٍ وَأُنثىٰ وَجَعَلناكُم شُعوبًا وَقَبائِلَ لِتَعارَفوا ۚ إِنَّ أَكرَمَكُم عِندَ اللَّهِ أَتقاكُم ۚ إِنَّ اللَّهَ عَليمٌ خَبيرٌ
>
> *Mankind! We created you from a male and female, and made you into peoples and tribes so that you might come to know each other. The noblest among you in Allāh's sight is the one with the most Taqwā. Allāh is All-Knowing, All-Aware.*[276]

Addressing mankind, Allāh informs us that He created us from water emerging from man and woman, or from Adam and Eve (*Hawā'*).[277,278] He made us close and distant relatives of one another, called 'tribes' (*Qabā'il*) and 'nations' (*Shuʿūb*). All people are equal as far as the nobility of the clay they were created from is concerned.[279] The only reason He made us such is that we recognise our close and distant relatives. It is not for the sake of declaring our superiority or determining our closeness to Allāh, for the closest to Allāh and the *noblest of you* (*Akramukum*) – if you

[276] Al-Qur'ān 49:13
[277] *Jāmiʿ al-Bayān fī Ta'wīl al-Qur'ān* – Imām al-Ṭabarī
[278] *Tafsīr al-Qur'ān al-ʿAẓīm* – Ibn Kathīr
[279] *Tafsīr al-Qur'ān al-ʿAẓīm* – Ibn Kathīr

insist on competing for nobility – are those who have the most Taqwā. The use of the restriction *'in Allāh's sight'* (*ʿind Allāh*) emphasises that no other criterion bears weight or value in His Sight.

'Allāh is All-Knowing, All-Aware.' Allāh knows well what true nobility is, and it is not the petty things like wealth or power. Allāh knows well who among you has the most Taqwā and thus who is the noblest in His Sight, because He is fully acquainted with your affairs. Nothing of this is hidden from Him.[280,281]

The determination of nobility follows verses concerning contempt and backbiting as both of these are attempts at sequestering one another's nobility. Since people are equal in their humanity with the only basis for nobility being Taqwā, which is hidden, attempts at belittling one's sibling are in vain. If the extent of one's Taqwā is hidden, it logically follows that one's true nobility is also hidden. And if one cannot ascertain their own level of Taqwā or nobility, then how then can one, through contempt, assume it absent from someone else? Ponder over the verse when Allāh says:

> هُوَ أَعْلَمُ بِكُمْ إِذْ أَنشَأَكُم مِّنَ الْأَرْضِ وَإِذْ أَنتُمْ أَجِنَّةٌ فِي بُطُونِ أُمَّهَاتِكُمْ ۖ فَلَا تُزَكُّوا أَنفُسَكُمْ ۖ هُوَ أَعْلَمُ بِمَنِ اتَّقَىٰ
>
> *He has the most knowledge of you when* ***He first produced you from the earth****, and when you were embryos in your mothers' wombs. So do not claim purity for yourselves. He knows best those who have Taqwā.*[282]

Peasant and king, learned and lay, poor and rich; He created us all from the same earth we wash off our clothes and trample on. Then we became feeble embryos, sitting in our mothers' wombs, dependant on their food, blood, and oxygen. As such, do not distinguish yourselves on the basis of the origin of your creation, as there is nothing exquisite or distinctive about it. The distinction of our nations and tribes is not to determine superiority but for the sole purpose of recognition. By turning this purpose and natural disposition (*Fitrah*) back to front, we turn what was intended for *recognition* (*Taʿāruf*) into a cause of *oblivion* (*Inkār*) and enmity.[283] And Allāh knows best those who have Taqwā.

---

[280] *Jāmiʿ al-Bayān fī Ta'wīl al-Qur'ān* – Imām al-Ṭabarī
[281] *Tafsīr al-Taḥrīr wa al-Tanwīr* – Ibn ʿĀshūr
[282] Al-Qur'ān 53:32
[283] *Tafsīr al-Taḥrīr wa al-Tanwīr* – Ibn ʿĀshūr

The Distinction of 'Taqwā' from the Sunnah

The Messenger of Allāh ﷺ was asked:

> أَيُّ النَّاسِ أَكْرَمُ؟ قَالَ، أَكْرَمُهُمْ عِنْدَ اللَّهِ أَتْقَاهُمْ. قَالُوا، لَيْسَ عَنْ هَذَا نَسْأَلُكَ. قَالَ، فَأَكْرَمُ النَّاسِ
> يُوسُفُ نَبِيُّ اللَّهِ، ابْنُ نَبِيِّ اللَّهِ، ابْنِ خَلِيلِ اللَّهِ. قَالُوا، لَيْسَ عَنْ هَذَا نَسْأَلُكَ. قَالَ، فَعَنْ مَعَادِنِ
> الْعَرَبِ تَسْأَلُونِي؟ قَالُوا، نَعَمْ. قَالَ، فَخِيَارُكُمْ فِي الْجَاهِلِيَّةِ خِيَارُكُمْ فِي الْإِسْلَامِ إِذَا فَقِهُوا

"Who are the noblest of the people?" The Prophet ﷺ said, "The noblest of them in Allāh's Sight are those with the most Taqwā." They said, "We do not ask you about that." He said, "Then the noblest of the people is Joseph (Yusuf), Allāh's prophet, the son of Allāh's prophet (Ya'qūb), the son of Allāh's prophet (Isḥāq), the son of Allāh's Khalīl (Ibrāhīm)." They said, "We do not ask you about that." The Prophet ﷺ said, "Do you ask about the virtues of the ancestry of the Arabs?" They said: "Yes." He ﷺ said, "Those who were the best amongst you in the pre-Islāmic period (Jāhiliyah) are the best amongst you in Islām if they comprehend [the Islāmic religion]."[284]

This means that if you insist on identifying the noblest ancestry then, so far as people's recognition is concerned, it is that which they recognised as being the noblest in the *Jāhiliyah*, for example, Banī Hāshim. This is on condition that they comprehend the religion of Allāh. All of this is secondary to the Prophet's first answer that the most honourable to Allāh is the one with the most Taqwā. The Prophet ﷺ further said:

> إِنَّ اللَّهَ لَا يَنْظُرُ إِلَى صُوَرِكُمْ وَأَمْوَالِكُمْ، وَلَكِنْ يَنْظُرُ إِلَى قُلُوبِكُمْ وَأَعْمَالِكُمْ

"Certainly, Allāh does not look to your faces and your wealth but He looks to your heart and to your deeds."[285]

In his sermon he delivered during the Farewell Pilgrimage, the Prophet ﷺ said:

---

[284] Ṣaḥīḥ Bukhārī on the authority of Abū Hurairah (raḍiy Allāhu 'anhu)
[285] Ṣaḥīḥ Muslim on the authority of Abū Hurairah (raḍiy Allāhu 'anhu)

> يا أيُّها النّاسُ ألا إنَّ ربَّكم واحِدٌ وأنَّ أباكم واحِدٌ لا فَضْلَ لِعَرَبِيٍّ عَلى عَجَمِيٍّ ولا لِعَجَمِيٍّ عَلى عَرَبِيٍّ ولا لِأسْوَدَ عَلى أحْمَرَ ولا لِأحْمَرَ عَلى أسْوَدَ إلّا بِالتَّقْوى
>
> *"O people, verily your Lord is One and your father is one. Verily there is no superiority of an Arab over a non-Arab or of a non-Arab over an Arab, or of a red man over a black man, or of a black man over a red man, except in terms of Taqwā."*[286]

The Prophet ﷺ delivered this emphatic statement during Ḥajj, which is an event that exemplifies it in both meaning and practice. Of every other issue the Prophet could have chosen as his parting advice, he chose this, beyond which the revelation would cease forever. This surely deserves a moment of deliberation.

The Honour of a Muslim from the Sunnah

ʿAbdullāh b. ʿUmar narrates that he saw the Prophet ﷺ making Ṭawāf around the Kaʿbah whilst saying:

> مَا أَطْيَبَكِ وَأَطْيَبَ رِيحَكِ، مَا أَعْظَمَكِ وَأَعْظَمَ حُرْمَتَكِ. وَالَّذِي نَفْسُ مُحَمَّدٍ بِيَدِهِ، لَحُرْمَةُ الْمُؤْمِنِ أَعْظَمُ عِنْدَ اللَّهِ حُرْمَةً مِنْكِ، مَالُهُ وَدَمُهُ، وَأَنْ نَظُنَّ بِهِ إِلَّا خَيْرًا
>
> *"How good you are and how good is your fragrance; how great you are and how great is your sanctity. By the One in Whose Hand is the soul of Muḥammad, the sanctity of the believer is greater before Allāh than your sanctity, his blood and his wealth, and that we think anything but good of him (the believer)."*[287]

The Prophet of Allāh ﷺ also said:

---

[286] Aḥmad on the authority of Abū Nadrah who relates the ḥadīth from those who heard the Prophet's farewell Khutbah

[287] *Ṣaḥīḥ* due to its supporting narrations – (classed *Ṣaḥīḥ* by al-Albani in *Ṣaḥīḥ al-Targhīb*), on the authority of ʿAbdullāh b. ʿUmar (raḍiy Allāhu ʿanhu)

> إِيَّاكُمْ وَالظَّنَّ فَإِنَّ الظَّنَّ أَكْذَبُ الْحَدِيثِ، وَلَا تَجَسَّسُوا وَلَا تَحَسَّسُوا، وَلَا تَنَافَسُوا، وَلَا تَحَاسَدُوا، وَلَا تَبَاغَضُوا، وَلَا تَدَابَرُوا، وَكُونُوا عِبَادَ اللَّهِ إِخْوَانًا
>
> *"Beware of suspicion. Suspicion is the most untrue speech. Do not spy. Do not compete with each other, do not envy each other, do not hate each other and do not shun each other. Be slaves of Allāh, brothers."*[288]

And he said:

> لَا تَقَاطَعُوا، وَلَا تَدَابَرُوا، وَلَا تَبَاغَضُوا، وَلَا تَحَاسَدُوا، وَكُونُوا عِبَادَ اللَّهِ إِخْوَانًا، وَلَا يَحِلُّ لِلْمُسْلِمِ أَنْ يَهْجُرَ أَخَاهُ فَوْقَ ثَلَاثَةِ أَيَّامٍ
>
> *"Do not cut off one another, nor desert one another, nor hate one another, nor envy one another. Be slaves of Allāh, brothers. It is not lawful for the Muslim to shun his brother for more than three days."*[289]

And during his farewell sermon the Prophet ﷺ said:

> إِنَّ دِمَاءَكُمْ وَأَمْوَالَكُمْ وَأَعْرَاضَكُمْ عَلَيْكُمْ حَرَامٌ، كَحُرْمَةِ يَوْمِكُمْ هَذَا، فِي شَهْرِكُمْ هَذَا، فِي بَلَدِكُمْ هَذَا
>
> *"Verily your blood, your property, and your honour are as sacred and inviolable as the sanctity of this day of yours, in this month of yours, and in this town of yours."*[290]

And he said:

> يا مَعْشَرَ مَنْ آمَنَ بِلِسَانِهِ وَلَمْ يَدْخُلِ الْإِيمَانُ قلبه، لا تغتابوا المسلمين، ولا تتبعوا عوراتهم، فَإِنَّهُ مَنْ يَتْبَعْ عَوْرَاتِهِمْ يَتْبَعِ اللَّهُ عَوْرَتَهُ وَمَنْ يَتْبَعِ اللَّهُ عَوْرَتَهُ يَفْضَحْهُ فِي بَيْتِهِ
>
> *"You who have [claimed] Imān by your tongue, but Imān has yet to enter their hearts, do not backbite Muslims, and do not search for their faults, for if anyone*

---

[288] *Ṣaḥīḥ* Bukhārī on the authority of Abū Hurairah (raḍiy Allāhu ʿanhu)
[289] *Ṣaḥīḥ* Bukhārī on the authority of Anas b. Mālik (raḍiy Allāhu ʿanhu)
[290] *Ṣaḥīḥ* Bukhārī and Muslim on the authority of Abu Bakrah (raḍiy Allāhu ʿanhu)

> *searches for their faults, Allāh will search for his fault, and if Allāh searches for the fault of anyone, He disgraces him in his very house."*[291]

The Prophet ﷺ warned:

> لَمَّا عُرِجَ بِي مَرَرْتُ بِقَوْمٍ لَهُمْ أَظْفَارٌ مِنْ نُحَاسٍ، يَخْمُشُونَ وُجُوهَهُمْ وَصُدُورَهُمْ، قُلْتُ، مَنْ هَؤُلَاءِ يَا جِبْرَائِيلُ؟ قَالَ، هَؤُلَاءِ الَّذِينَ يَأْكُلُونَ لُحُومَ النَّاسِ، وَيَقَعُونَ فِي أَعْرَاضِهِمْ
>
> *"During the Miʿrāj (the Night of Ascension), I saw a group of people who were scratching their chests and faces with their copper nails. I asked, 'Who are these people, O Jibrīl?' Jibrīl replied, 'These are the people who ate flesh of others [by backbiting] and trampled people's honour.'"*[292]

Reasons for Revelation

Reports suggest that the verse prohibiting ridicule was revealed on account of some of the Prophet's wives making fun of Umm Salamah's shortness, or of others calling Safiyyah, the daughter of Huyay (from Khaybar), a 'Jewish lady'. Both stemmed from the natural jealousy that would sometimes overtake our mothers' actions and words, not least that Safiyyah (raḍiy Allāhu ʿanhā) was from noble ancestry.[293]

Others said that at least part of verse 11 was revealed concerning a Madani tribe by the name of Banī Salamah. When they accepted Islām upon the arrival of the Messenger of Allāh ﷺ, many were still being referred to by the nicknames they had inherited from the days of pre-Islāmic ignorance. Many disliked to be called by these former nicknames.[294]

Other exegetes mention that the companion Thābit b. Qais suffered from a weak sense of hearing so would sit at the very front of the Masjid to hear the Prophet ﷺ.[295] Once, Thābit entered the crowded Masjid wanting to sit at the front. As he shuffled through the rows, a man told him to sit where he was, refusing to make way for Thābit. Frustrated, Thābit sat behind the man. After some time, Thābit asked the man, "*Who are you*?" The man replied, "*I am so and so.*" Thābit responded, "*The son of so and so woman?*" referring to him by the derogatory name people would give that man before his Islām. The man lowered his head ashamed. Al-Qurtubi adds that the Prophet ﷺ

---

[291] *Sunan* Abī Dāwūd on the authority of Abū Barzah al-Aslamī (raḍiy Allāhu ʿanhu)

[292] *Sunan* Abī Dāwūd on the authority of Anas b. Mālik (raḍiy Allāhu ʿanhu)

[293] *Al-Jāmiʿ li Aḥkām al-Qur'ān* – Imām Qurṭubī

[294] *Jāmiʿ al-Bayān fī Ta'wīl al-Qur'ān* – Imām al-Ṭabarī

[295] *Ma'ālim al-Tanzīl - al-Baghawī; al-Tashīl li 'Ulūm al-Tanzīl* – Ibn al-Jawzi; and others

asked, *"Who mentioned so and so woman?"* Thābit replied, *"Me, O Messenger of Allāh."* The Prophet said, *"Look at the faces around you."* Thābit looked and the Messenger continued, *"What did you see?"* He said, *"I see the white, the black and the red."* The Prophet said, *"You cannot be distinguished over them except by way of Taqwā."* As such, the verse was revealed concerning this incident.[296]

Concerning the verse of *Taqwā*, verse 13, it was reported that the Prophet ﷺ ordered a tribe by the name of Banī Bayādah from the *Anṣār* to marry a man by the name of Abu Hind to a woman from their tribe. Abu Hind was, however, one of their servants. They objected and said, *"How can we marry our daughters to our servants?"* Allāh then revealed the verse.

Others report that during the conquest of Makkah, the Prophet ﷺ instructed Bilāl (raḍiy Allāhu ʿanhu) to climb the Kaʿbah and deliver the Adhān. Some of those who had newly embraced Islām jeered that a black man who had once held the social status of a slave was now standing in the heart of Makkah, on top of the most sanctified house. It is said that when news of their mockery reached the Prophet, Allāh revealed the verse. And Allāh knows best.

[296] *Al-Jāmiʿ li Aḥkām al-Qur'ān* – Imām Qurṭubī

SECTION 5: THE REALITY OF *ĪMĀN* IN ALLĀH

In the previous section, Allāh outlined the ethics due towards Mu'minūn; both in their presence and in their absence, as well as those we should harbour internally. We concluded that the noblest among mankind are those with the most Taqwā. Since Taqwā is of the exclusive knowledge of Allāh, only He can determine true nobility. He is fully acquainted with what occurs in the hearts. Ultimately, none of these ethics can truly be realised or accepted by Allāh except with true Īmān and sincerity of intention. All of *al-Ḥujurāt*'s ethics and realisations are a consequence of one's internal sense of Īmān. Allāh's appeal to Īmān is repeated again and again because it is a requisite for every objective mannerism. Īmān is a remarkable inner and outer condition and, as such, far beyond a claim merely occurring on the tongue. It has fundamentals and stipulations and is validated by hard work and sacrifice. Al-Ḥasan al-Baṣrī is reported to have said:

> إن الإيمان ليس بالتحلي ولا بالتمني إن الإيمان ما وقر في القلب وصدقه العمل
>
> *"Īmān does not come through hopeful wishes nor [outer] decor. Īmān is what establishes itself in the heart and is validated by action."*

Verses 14-18

> قَالَتِ الْأَعْرَابُ آمَنَّا ۖ قُل لَّمْ تُؤْمِنُوا وَلَٰكِن قُولُوا أَسْلَمْنَا وَلَمَّا يَدْخُلِ الْإِيمَانُ فِي قُلُوبِكُمْ ۖ وَإِن تُطِيعُوا
> اللَّهَ وَرَسُولَهُ لَا يَلِتْكُم مِّنْ أَعْمَالِكُمْ شَيْئًا ۚ إِنَّ اللَّهَ غَفُورٌ رَّحِيمٌ ◊ إِنَّمَا الْمُؤْمِنُونَ الَّذِينَ آمَنُوا بِاللَّهِ

> وَرَسُولِهِ ثُمَّ لَمْ يَرْتَابُوا وَجَاهَدُوا بِأَمْوَالِهِمْ وَأَنفُسِهِمْ فِي سَبِيلِ اللَّهِ ۚ أُولَٰئِكَ هُمُ الصَّادِقُونَ ◇ قُلْ أَتُعَلِّمُونَ
> اللَّهَ بِدِينِكُمْ وَاللَّهُ يَعْلَمُ مَا فِي السَّمَاوَاتِ وَمَا فِي الْأَرْضِ ۚ وَاللَّهُ بِكُلِّ شَيْءٍ عَلِيمٌ ◇ يَمُنُّونَ عَلَيْكَ أَنْ
> أَسْلَمُوا ۖ قُل لَّا تَمُنُّوا عَلَيَّ إِسْلَامَكُم ۖ بَلِ اللَّهُ يَمُنُّ عَلَيْكُمْ أَنْ هَدَاكُمْ لِلْإِيمَانِ إِن كُنتُمْ صَادِقِينَ ◇
> إِنَّ اللَّهَ يَعْلَمُ غَيْبَ السَّمَاوَاتِ وَالْأَرْضِ ۚ وَاللَّهُ بَصِيرٌ بِمَا تَعْمَلُونَ
>
> *The desert Arabs say, "We have Īmān." Say, "You do not have Īmān."Rather, say, "We have become Muslim," for Īmān has not yet entered into your hearts. If you obey Allāh and His Messenger, He will not undervalue your actions in any way. Allāh is Ever-Forgiving, Most Merciful. The Mu'minūn'are only those who have had Īmān in Allāh and His Messenger and then have had no doubt and have done Jihād with their wealth and themselves in the Way of Allāh. They are the ones who are true to their word. Say, "Do you presume to teach Allāh your Dīn when Allāh knows everything in the Heavens and everything in the Earth? Allāh has knowledge of all things." They think they have done you a favour by becoming Muslims! Say, "Do not consider your Islām a favour to me. No indeed! It is Allāh who has favoured you by guiding you to Īmān if you are telling the truth."Allāh knows the unseen things of the Heavens and the Earth. Allāh sees what you do.*[297]

Verse 14:

> قَالَتِ الْأَعْرَابُ آمَنَّا ۖ قُل لَّمْ تُؤْمِنُوا وَلَٰكِن قُولُوا أَسْلَمْنَا وَلَمَّا يَدْخُلِ الْإِيمَانُ فِي قُلُوبِكُمْ ۖ وَإِن تُطِيعُوا
> اللَّهَ وَرَسُولَهُ لَا يَلِتْكُم مِّنْ أَعْمَالِكُمْ شَيْئًا ۚ إِنَّ اللَّهَ غَفُورٌ رَّحِيمٌ
>
> *The desert Arabs say, "We have Īmān." Say, "You do not have Īmān." Rather, say, "We have become Muslim," for Īmān has not yet entered into your hearts. If you obey Allāh and His Messenger, He will not undervalue your actions in any way. Allāh is Ever-Forgiving, Most Merciful.*[298]

[297] Al-Qur'ān 49:14-18
[298] Al-Qur'ān 49:14

Among the many delegations that came to Madīnah in the ninth year of Hijrah was a tribe by the name Banī Asad b. Khuzaimah, who arrived shortly after Banī Tamīm.[299] A drought had taken grip of their town and they naturally chose to escape and relocate to Madīnah to receive the Messenger's support. Others may have been more sincere in their coming. Addressing the noble Messenger ﷺ, they would say, *"The Arabs came as individuals on their rides but we came to you with all of our belongings and children and we did not fight you as so and so did..."*

Notice how *al-Ḥujurāt* coherently begins by addressing the behaviour of Banī Tamīm and concludes by addressing the behaviour of Banī Asad. In terms of associating the two accounts, both arrived to Madīnah at a similar time and the nature of their misbehaviour was very much the same.[300] Banī Tamīm raised their voices above the noble Messenger of Allāh ﷺ, expressively putting themselves *ahead*. They assumed themselves to be the worthy centre of priority and importance. Similarly, Banī Asad deemed their arrival *a favour* to the Messenger of Allāh ﷺ, suggesting the Messenger ﷺ and his mission had exclusively anticipated their arrival and was bolstered by their support. Their belief was that the ummah should be indebted to them.

The above verse is understood as follows:

'The Bedouins said we have Īmān in Allāh and His Messenger, therefore we are 'Mu'minūn'. Say, to them, Muḥammad ﷺ, you did not really have Īmān, nor are you 'Mu'minūn', but instead say 'we have become Muslim' (aslamnā).'

This is because Islām is confined to speech (which is all they brought), whereas Īmān is both speech and action and they had yet to support their claim to Islām with the necessary action. Another understanding considers the literal and linguistic meaning of 'Islām' – submission (istislām). Specifically, 'do not say 'āmannā'', but say 'we have submitted (istaslamnā)'. They submitted to the Messenger's ﷺ political strength and authority after fearing fighting him, being taken as captives, or being killed. Imām al-Ṭabarī prioritises the first meaning; that Allāh wished for their claim to be more precise. Instead of 'āmannā', specify it by either 'we have believed in Allāh and His Messenger ('āmannā billāhi warasūlih') or just say, 'aslamnā'. In other words, you have merely uttered the declaration (Shahādah or Kalimah). The knowledge of Īmān, its full meanings and implications are yet to enter your hearts.[301]

Note that saying 'has not yet' (*'Lamma'*) is different to saying 'has not' (*'Lam'*). *'Lam'* suggests a current and continuous negation, meaning that *'Īmān has still not entered your hearts'* and there is little hope of change in the future. *'Lamma'*,

---

[299] As explored in Section 1: Those who called out the Messenger, p. 51

[300] *Tafsīr al-Taḥrīr wa al-Tanwīr* – Ibn ʿĀshūr

[301] *Jāmiʿ al-Bayān fī Ta'wīl al-Qur'ān* – Imām al-Ṭabarī

however, suggests negation that is likely to change in the future. Therefore, though it is true that Īmān has not *yet* entered your hearts, this is likely to change if you exert the necessary effort.[302] It could also be that the Bedouins had not had Īmān when they claimed they had, only to become Mu'minūn afterwards. The statement, *'you do not have Īmān'* is a very startling exposition that could have convinced them that their Lord knows the unseen (*Ghayb*). Thus, the exposition, *'you do not have Īmān'* could be exactly what fostered Īmān in their hearts.[303]

· *'If you obey Allāh and His Messenger, He will not undervalue your actions in any way. Allāh is Ever-Forgiving, Most Merciful.'* If you obey Allāh and His Messenger, carry out their commands and abstain from their prohibitions, the reward of your actions will not be diminished in the least, and your favour of having come to Islām without fighting the Muslims – as you assert – will be to your credit.[304] Your cure is to spend some time learning from the Prophet ﷺ the true dictates of Īmān during your stay in Madīnah rather than boasting and asking for money.

After doing this, Allāh is Oft-Forgiving (*Ghafūr*) towards those who obey Him. He is also Merciful (*Raḥīm*) towards His creatures who repent such that He will not punish them for those sins they have repented from.[305] *Ghafūr* and *Raḥīm* are in the hyperbolised forms. Allāh will not only forgive a person's bad actions before Islām as soon as they accept Islām, but He will also reward a person for the good actions they did before their Islām as well.

Your Reality Will Be Exposed by Allāh

What is clear from this verse and others is that Allāh will ultimately bring out a person's reality on their tongue and in their actions. If Īmān, sincerity, truthfulness, righteousness, or any other positive trait remains as lip service, know that it *will* be tested such that its truth will be exposed. Allāh says:

> الم ◊ أَحَسِبَ النَّاسُ أَن يُتْرَكُوا أَن يَقُولُوا آمَنَّا وَهُمْ لَا يُفْتَنُونَ ◊ وَلَقَدْ فَتَنَّا الَّذِينَ مِن قَبْلِهِمْ فَلَيَعْلَمَنَّ
> اللَّهُ الَّذِينَ صَدَقُوا وَلَيَعْلَمَنَّ الْكَاذِبِينَ

[302] *Al-Kashāf* – al-Zamakhshari; and others
[303] *Tafsīr al-Ḥujurāt* – Muḥammad Metwalī al-Sha'rāwī
[304] *Jāmi' al-Bayān fī Ta'wīl al-Qur'ān* – Imām al-Ṭabarī
[305] *Tafsīr al-Taḥrīr wa al-Tanwīr* – Ibn 'Āshūr

> *Do people imagine that they will be left to say, "We have Īmān," and will not be tested? We tested those before them so that Allāh would know the truthful and would know the liars.*[306]

Ibn ʿAbbas (raḍiy Allāhu ʿanhu) reports that Allāh's Messenger ﷺ said:

> مَنْ سَمَّعَ سَمَّعَ اللَّهُ بِهِ وَمَنْ رَاءَى رَاءَى اللَّهُ بِه
>
> *"If anyone desires to be heard, Allāh will publicise [his humiliation]. And if anyone desires to be seen [doing good deeds], Allāh will make a display of him."*[307]

This terrifying reality is again explained by the dictates of 'you reap what you sow' (*al-jazāʾu min jins al ʿamāl*). It is a serious warning that should remind us to work hard on our intentions and purposes. Today's world is overshadowed by superficial displays of righteousness and da'wah, propelled by addictive social media recognition and popularity. How many of us interrogate ourselves as to whether we are truly speaking on behalf of Allāh, seeking His pleasure and positive reform on Earth, or whether we are simply riding the popularity wave and auditioning for Islāmic celebrity status?

Today, it is alarming to see a huge number of du'āt falling victim to people's expectations and hence not coming out strong regarding the most important matters for fear of losing their positions, platforms or popularity, or fearing the reaction of those in power. The verse highlights how one's reputation can be tarnished through their very attempt to protect it. How many, fearing for their comfort, are today providing religious justification for the abominations committed by their pseudo-religious authorities, only for their inconsistencies to appear as bright as the sun and be called out by common Muslims? The Prophet ﷺ said:

> مَنِ الْتَمَسَ رِضَى اللَّهِ بِسَخَطِ النَّاسِ، رَضِيَ الله عَنْهُ، وَأَرْضَى النَّاسَ عَنْهُ، وَمَنِ الْتَمَسَ رِضَا النَّاسِ بِسَخَطِ اللَّهِ ، سَخَطَ اللَّهُ عَلَيْهِ ، وَأَسْخَطَ عليه الناس
>
> *"Whoever seeks the pleasure of Allāh at the expense of people's displeasure, Allāh will be pleased with him and Allāh will make the people pleased with him. And*

---

306 Al-Qur'ān 29:1-2

307 *Ṣaḥīḥ* Muslim on the authority of ʿAbdullāh b. ʿAbbas (raḍiy Allāhu ʿanhu)

> *whoever seeks the pleasure of people at the expense of Allāh's pleasure, Allāh will be displeased with him and will make the people displeased with him."*[308]

The forthcoming verses of *al-Ḥujurāt* address 'performances' during comfortable and secure times, revealing that it is during testing times that true and sincere Mu'minūn are known; those who, in adversity, surrender their wealth, reputation, freedom and even their own selves for the sake of Allāh; those who, as followers of Muḥammad ﷺ, declare an unwavering pledge though alone and isolated, just as he did during those arduous days at the very beginning of Prophethood:

> والله لو وضعوا الشمس في يميني، والقمر في يساري على أن أترك هذا الأمر حتى يظهره الله، أو أهلك فيه، ما تركته
>
> *"By Allāh, if they were to put the sun in my right and the moon in my left in return that I leave this matter (Islām), I will not leave it until it prevails or I die upon that."*[309]

Even if Banī Asad were to give their lives for the cause of Islām, still, gratitude would solely be due to Allāh since Allāh gave them those lives and that wealth about which they boast. They are, moreover, merely doing that which will bring them benefit in the hereafter. They are also the first beneficiaries of the societal ethics outlined in *al-Ḥujurāt* they subscribe to by joining the Messenger's ﷺ community. Just as they should not ridicule, find fault, call names, hold bad suspicion, spy, and backbite, they are now protected from such evils from the rest of society.

As we mentioned when elucidating the meaning of Allāh's *Faḍl*, He gave, then rewarded for what He gave. After they die as Mu'minūn, their destination will be Paradise for doing what ultimately benefitted them to begin with. And all praise and thanks are due to Allāh alone.

---

[308] Ibn Hibbān on the authority of ʿĀ'ishah (raḍiy Allāhu ʿanhā)

[309] *Sīrah* – Ibn Hishām

ARE YOU A 'MUSLIM BY NAME'?

A person seldom struggles and sacrifices for something he or she does not believe in wholeheartedly. On the contrary, those who work hard, struggle, and fight for the sake of their Islām have truly proven to have overcome their own inclinations. This is because that person will have put at stake their *Nafs* (self) which commands them towards desires and inclinations. Those who harbour doubts in their Īmān will simply not struggle against others to defend or spread that frailty. The truthful ones (*Ṣādiqūn*) are those who have validated their verbal claims with action.

It comes as no surprise that giving charity is called *Ṣadaqah* – from the root of 'truth' or 'validation' (*Taṣdīq*), for it is a direct, tangible validator of Īmān – to give up what you love. Unsurprisingly, in the Qur'ān, of the most consistent and defining characteristic of the hypocrites – those whose outer conditions are invalidated or belied (*Takdhīb*) by their inner – is their tight-fistedness. Allāh says:

> الْمُنَافِقُونَ وَالْمُنَافِقَاتُ بَعْضُهُم مِّن بَعْضٍ ۚ يَأْمُرُونَ بِالْمُنكَرِ وَيَنْهَوْنَ عَنِ الْمَعْرُوفِ وَيَقْبِضُونَ أَيْدِيَهُمْ
>
> *The men and women of the hypocrites are as bad as one another. They command what is wrong and forbid what is right and keep their fists tightly closed.*[310]

And:

> هُمُ الَّذِينَ يَقُولُونَ لَا تُنفِقُوا عَلَىٰ مَنْ عِندَ رَسُولِ اللَّهِ حَتَّىٰ يَنفَضُّوا ۗ وَلِلَّهِ خَزَائِنُ السَّمَاوَاتِ وَالْأَرْضِ
> وَلَٰكِنَّ الْمُنَافِقِينَ لَا يَفْقَهُونَ
>
> *They are the people who say, "Do not spend on those who are with the Messenger of Allāh, so that they may go away." The treasuries of the Heavens and Earth belong to Allāh. But the hypocrites do not understand this.*[311]

Among many other verses containing a similar meaning. Conversely:

---

[310] Al-Qur'ān 9:67
[311] Al-Qur'ān 63:7

Verse 15:

> إِنَّمَا الْمُؤْمِنُونَ الَّذِينَ آمَنُوا بِاللَّهِ وَرَسُولِهِ ثُمَّ لَمْ يَرْتَابُوا وَجَاهَدُوا بِأَمْوَالِهِمْ وَأَنفُسِهِمْ فِي سَبِيلِ اللَّهِ ۚ أُولَٰئِكَ
> هُمُ الصَّادِقُونَ
>
> *The Mu'minūn are only those who have had Īmān in Allāh and His Messenger and then have had no doubt and have done Jihād with their wealth and themselves in the Way of Allāh. They are the ones who are true to their word.*[312]

The Mu'minūn are those who have Īmān in Allāh and His Messenger, hold no doubts in their Īmān and strive (*Jāhadū*) with their wealth and lives for the sake of Allāh. They are the ones sincere in their claim to Īmān, having verified their words with action.[313] The first word 'only' (*innamā*), formulates a restrictive sentence (*Haṣr*), so as to say that the Mu'minūn are 'none but' those who truly possess Īmān in Allāh and His Messenger without harbouring doubts, and 'none but' those who have striven.[314] This subtly indicates that the Bedouins who claimed Īmān may have continued to harbour doubts and that the Īmān in their hearts was still fragile and unsteady. This is not to say that they were intentionally lying, as if that were the case they would have been called out as hypocrites.[315]

Likewise, the Mu'minūn are those who impose on themselves obedience to Allāh and His Messenger without doubting the binding nature of their commands. They are those who '*Jāhadū*', encompassing, where applicable, the action of fighting the Mushrikīn with both their wealth and their selves such that Allāh's Word is raised above every other. [316]

Verse 16:

> قُلْ أَتُعَلِّمُونَ اللَّهَ بِدِينِكُمْ وَاللَّهُ يَعْلَمُ مَا فِي السَّمَاوَاتِ وَمَا فِي الْأَرْضِ ۚ وَاللَّهُ بِكُلِّ شَيْءٍ عَلِيمٌ

312 Al-Qur'ān 49:15
313 *Jāmi' al-Bayān fī Ta'wīl al-Qur'ān* – Imām al-Ṭabarī
314 *Tafsīr al-Taḥrīr wa al-Tanwīr* – Ibn 'Āshūr
315 *Tafsīr al-Qur'ān al-'Aẓīm* – Ibn Kathīr
316 *Jāmi' al-Bayān fī Ta'wīl al-Qur'ān* – Imām al-Ṭabarī

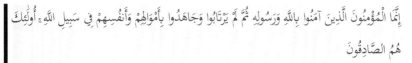

> *Say, "Do you presume to teach Allāh your Dīn when Allāh knows everything in the Heavens and everything in the Earth? Allāh has knowledge of all things.'"*[317]

Say, O Muḥammad to these Bedouins, are you teaching Allāh about your religion (i.e., about the extent of your obedience) (*Dīn*) when Allāh knows everything in the seven Heavens and Earth?[318] Notice that 'are you *teaching*' (*atuʿalimūn*) has been used as opposed to 'are you *informing*' (*atukhbirūn*). This is because teaching involves an emphasised effort of convincing the listener with evidence and persistence. It is as if to say, 'are you insisting on trying to convince the Prophet of something Allāh certainly *knows* to be false?'[319] Nothing is hidden from Him, so how could the condition of your Īmān be hidden from Him? *'Allāh has knowledge of all things'*, so be cautious of saying with your tongues the opposite of what is in your hearts.

Verse 17:

> يَمُنُّونَ عَلَيْكَ أَنْ أَسْلَمُوا ۖ قُل لَّا تَمُنُّوا عَلَيَّ إِسْلَامَكُم ۖ بَلِ اللَّهُ يَمُنُّ عَلَيْكُمْ أَنْ هَدَاكُمْ لِلْإِيمَانِ إِن كُنتُمْ صَادِقِينَ
>
> *They think they have done you a favour by becoming Muslims! Say, "Do not consider your Islām a favour to me. No indeed! It is Allāh who has favoured you by guiding you to Īmān if you are telling the truth."*[320]

To add to the falseness of their claim, they see it a favour on you that they have become Muslims. *'Mann'* (from *'yamunnūna'*) is when one articulates their favours and acts of goodness, anticipating renumeration from the recipient or otherwise. It can either be direct or indirect. Direct *'Mann'* is to state your favour and your anticipation of remuneration explicitly. In the case of Banī Asad, they said, "*We did not fight you as did so and so.*" Indirect *'Mann'* is to hide it such that it sounds like one is merely conveying information. Again, in the case of Banī Asad, they said, "*We came to you with our children and belongings,*"[321] which is an evident reality, and is thus an

[317] Al-Qur'ān 49:16
[318] *Jāmiʿ al-Bayān fī Ta'wīl al-Qur'ān* – Imām al-Ṭabarī
[319] *Tafsīr al-Taḥrīr wa al-Tanwīr* – Ibn ʿĀshūr
[320] Al-Qur'ān 49:17
[321] *Tafsīr al-Taḥrīr wa al-Tanwīr* – Ibn ʿĀshūr

obvious request for requital. Tell them, O Muḥammad, *"do not consider your Islām a favour to me"* for it is Allāh who has favoured you and gifted you by guiding you to Īmān in Allāh and His Messenger, if you are really telling the truth about having become Mu'minūn.[322]

Claiming Īmān or denying it from others who have claimed it is an attempt to teach Allāh about what is in people's hearts. This is of the worst manners a person can have towards His Creator and an evident example of *putting oneself ahead of Allāh*. From this perspective, we notice the cyclical structure of the *Sūrah* as it returns to its beginning in relation to manners with Allāh (*'do not put yourselves forward in front of Allāh'*), bringing *al-Ḥujurāt*'s central messages to a close in the most spectacular way.[323]

If you are not attempting to teach Allāh the covert matters of Īmān, then the alternative is that you are doing *'Mann'* to His Messenger, proving the aforesaid. You are putting him under the obligation of showing you gratitude. It is as if the Bedouins said, "We have given up a lot for you." In reality, you have done no favour for the Messenger of Allāh ﷺ. Instead, Allāh has done a favour for you for which you should be grateful.

Verse 18:

> إِنَّ اللَّهَ يَعْلَمُ غَيْبَ السَّمَاوَاتِ وَالْأَرْضِ ۚ وَاللَّهُ بَصِيرٌ بِمَا تَعْمَلُونَ
>
> *Allāh knows the unseen things of the Heavens and the Earth. Allāh sees what you do.*[324]

He knows the truthful one from the liar. He knows those who have become Muslim desiring the Face of Allāh and those who have done so fearing His Messenger ﷺ.[325]

This reference to the Heavens and Earth differs from that in verse 16. Verse 16 may imply in the minds of some that Allāh's knowledge is limited to that which is known by us or is accessible. Verse 18 affirms that Allāh's knowledge extends to the *unseen*. Allāh employs the emphatic device *'inna'* (*surely* or *most certainly*) to address the doubt in this reality the Bedouins expressed by their actions.[326]

---

[322] *Jāmiʿ al-Bayān fī Ta'wīl al-Qur'ān* – Imām al-Ṭabarī
[323] *Taysīr al-Karīm al-Raḥmān fī Tafsīr Kalām al-Mannān* – ʿAbdur-Raḥmān Al-Saʿdī
[324] Al-Qur'ān 49:18
[325] *Jāmiʿ al-Bayān fī Ta'wīl al-Qur'ān* – Imām al-Ṭabarī
[326] *Tafsīr al-Taḥrīr wa al-Tanwīr* – Ibn ʿĀshūr

Do not teach Allāh the secrets of your hearts, for there are secrets in the Heavens and Earth that Allāh knows and has hidden from you. *'Allāh sees what you do'*, so do not suppose that Allāh's knowledge of secret and hidden matters means He does not see what is open and revealed. He sees both your secret and open matters, and will reward or punish accordingly.[327] Reflect on the relevance of this to the verse of *Taqwā* and how often our acts of ridicule, name-calling, bad-suspicion and so on imply we deign to teach Allāh about who has Taqwā and who does not.

Greatness within Greatness

Allāh speaks of the Heavens and the Earth in three distinct ways, embracing everything in existence, both seen and hidden. The first is that He possesses (*lahū*) the entire dominion (*Mulk*) of the Heavens and Earth. The second is that He knows, possesses and owns what and who is *within* (*mā fī* and *man fī*) the Heavens and the Earth. The third is that *'He knows the unseen things of the Heavens and the Earth,'* and *'the Unseen of the Heavens and the Earth belongs to Him.'*

The Heavens and the Earth are astonishing in and of themselves, yet Allāh makes reference to *'what is in the Heavens and the Earth.'* Whilst we are impressed by the visible, extraordinary and vast Heavens and Earth, we recognise that the contents of an envelope or canopy are more significant and incredible than the envelope itself. There must exist amazing, undiscovered treasures enveloped within amazing, known riches, enveloped by the expansive Heaven and the Earth canopy. All aspects are individually astonishing, eminent and magnificent (*'aẓīm*). The dimension of the unseen (*Ghayb*) is expansive beyond limits. We will continuously discover as Allāh allows segments of the *Ghayb* to transition from the hidden dimension to the revealed.[328] Everything we discover of the hidden, including the hidden treasures of the Qur'ān, will invariably testify to its truth:

> سَنُرِيهِمْ آيَاتِنَا فِي الْآفَاقِ وَفِي أَنفُسِهِمْ حَتَّىٰ يَتَبَيَّنَ لَهُمْ أَنَّهُ الْحَقُّ ۗ أَوَلَمْ يَكْفِ بِرَبِّكَ أَنَّهُ عَلَىٰ كُلِّ شَيْءٍ شَهِيدٌ
>
> *We will show them Our Signs on the horizon and within themselves until it is clear to them that it is the truth. Is it not enough for your Lord that He is a witness of everything?*[329]

[327] *Jāmi' al-Bayān fī Ta'wīl al-Qur'ān* – Imām al-Ṭabarī
[328] *Tafsīr al-Ḥujurāt* – Muḥammad Metwalī al-Sha'rāwī
[329] Al-Qur'ān 41:53

The Difference between Īmān and Islām

In the previous verses, we see references to both Īmān and Islām. What is the difference between the two? In general, *'Īmān'* is more specific than Islām. This is evidenced in the ḥadīth of Jibrīl (ʿalayhi al-Salām) when he asked the Prophet ﷺ about *'Islām'*, then about *'Īmān'*, then about *'Iḥsān'* (perfection), transitioning each time from the general to the more specific:

> يا محمدُ، أخبرني عن الإسلامِ. فقال رسولُ اللهِ صلى الله عليه وسلم، الإسلامُ أن تَشْهَدَ أن لا إلهَ إلا اللهُ وأن محمدًا رسولُ الله، وتُقيمَ الصلاةُ، وتُؤْتِيَ الزكاةَ، وتَصومَ رمضانَ، وتَحُجَّ البيتَ إن استطعْتَ إليه سبيلًا. قال، صدقْتَ. قال، فعجِبْنا له يَسْأَلُه ويُصَدِّقُه. قال، فأخبرْني عن الإيمانِ. قال، أن تُؤْمِنَ باللهِ، وملائكتِه، وكتبِه، ورسلِه، واليومِ الآخرِ، وتؤمنَ بالقدرِ خيرِه وشرِّه. قال، صدَقْتَ. قال، فأخبرْني عن الإحسانِ. قال، أن تَعْبُدَ اللهَ كأنك تراه، فإن لم تَكُنْ تراه فإنه يراك
>
> *"O Muḥammad ﷺ! Tell me about Islām." The Messenger of Allāh ﷺ replied, "Islām is* ***to testify*** *that none has the right to be worshipped but Allāh, and that Muḥammad is the Messenger of Allāh; that you* ***observe Ṣalāt, pay Zakāt, observe fasting*** *of Ramaḍān and* ***perform Ḥajj*** *of the House, provided you have resources of making journey to it." He [Jibrīl (ʿalayhi al-Salām)] replied, "You have spoken the truth." We were surprised to see that he had asked him and confirmed the correctness of the answers. He then enquired, "Tell me about Īmān." He ﷺ said, "It is to believe in Allāh, His Angels, His Books, His Messengers, the Last Day, and that you believe in preordainment (destiny), [both] its bad and good consequences." He said, "You have spoken the truth." He then enquired, "Tell me about Iḥsān." He ﷺ said, "It is to worship Allāh as if you are seeing Him, and although you do not see Him, He sees you."*[330,331]

We learn from this ḥadīth that *'Islām'*, when differentiated from *'Īmān'*, comprises the actions of the tongue and those of the limbs, i.e., the 'Five Pillars of Islām'. *Īmān*, on the other hand, involves internalising the belief system wholeheartedly in a way

---

[330] *Ṣaḥīḥ* Muslim on the authority of ʿUmar b. al-Khaṭṭab (raḍiy Allāhu ʿanhu)

[331] *Tafsīr al-Qur'ān al-ʿAẓīm* – Ibn Kathīr

that drives those actions, but with greater conscious internal conviction. Then the innermost sphere of *Iḥsān* is to worship Allāh as if you see Him, which is the ultimate distinction and the highest level possible a Muslim can reach. Just below this, within the outer sphere of *Iḥsān*, is to worship Allāh with the conviction that He can see you, while begetting the associated effects of this on the quality of your worship.

The definitions of Islām and Īmān will usually assume the aforementioned distinct meanings when mentioned *side by side* as in the case of *al-Ḥujurāt*. In the case of verses 14-17, Allāh clearly distinguishes between the two terms. Islām and Īmān can, however, assume the same meaning if occurring entirely separately. For instance, there is no doubt that when Allāh says, *'You who have Īmān'*, with no mention of Islām in *al-Ḥujurāt* or elsewhere, it simultaneously addresses Muslims in name as well as those who are Mu'min and Muḥsin. May Allāh grant us the sweetness of Īmān.

TO WHOM DO WE *TRULY* OWE GRATITUDE?

It is said that the Bedouins of Banī Asad who arrived professing their Islām would throw their rubbish in the walkways of Madīnah. Their surge on the markets also inflated the prices of Madīnah's commodities. Despite this, they would plead for *Ṣadaqah*, reasoning that they came as *Mu'minūn* carrying all their belongings to Madīnah, and that they did not fight the Prophet ﷺ as others did.

Gratitude is Entirely Due to Allāh and His Messenger

Principled societies recognise that the son or daughter is obliged to obey their parents, knowing well that they will never be able to repay their favours. It is discourteous enough that the child perceives their service and obedience to their parents a favour in his or her parents' twilight years. Image, then, if the person demands gratitude despite being the persistent recipient of a favour. Imagine a nursing baby demanding gratitude from his or her mother?

Likewise, nothing can meet the Prophet's favour towards us. If having *everything* besides the Prophet's guidance does not earn one salvation, it follows that the Prophet's guidance is much more valuable than *everything*. As such, no level of gratitude or service can truly match it.

During the Battle of Hunayn, one year before Banī Asad boasted about their Īmān, the Prophet ﷺ distributed the spoils between members of Quraish and other Arab tribes who were new Muslims, leaving *nothing* for the Anṣār. Let us take a moment here to recall who the *Anṣār* were. Besides their deal to protect the Prophet ﷺ, they were unexpectedly confronted with some 1,000 soldiers who sought nothing less than their eradication. Representing the Anṣār, Saʿd b. Muʿādh (raḍiy Allāhu ʿanhu), with the knowledge that he might commit the *whole* contingent of the Anṣār to the prospect of martyrdom, got up and declared:

> لقد آمنا بك وصدقناك، وشهدنا أن ما جئت به هو الحق، وأعطيناك على ذلك عهودنا ومواثيقنا،
> فامض يا رسول الله لما أردت، فنحن معك، فوالذي بعثك بالحق لو استعرضت بنا هذا البحر،
> فخضته لخضناه معك، ما تخلف منا رجل واحد
>
> *"We believed (Āmannā) in you, we declare your truth, and we witness that what you have brought us is the truth, and we have given you our word and agreement to*

> *hear and obey; so go wherever you wish, we are with you. By He who sent you, if you were to ask us to cross this sea and you plunged into it, we would plunge into it with you; not a man would stay behind."*[332]

It was the Anṣār who hosted the Messenger of Allāh ﷺ and surrendered everything for him after he was exiled from Makkah and violently banished from Ṭa'if. In Uḥud, when the tables turned in favour of Quraish, it was the phenomenally gallant Anṣār who planted themselves firmly around the Messenger ﷺ. Out of the 70 companions who were martyred in the Battle of Uḥud, almost all were from the Anṣār. They were the generous hosts of the Muhājirūn; they sacrificed their homes and livelihoods for them and expected no renumeration. And yet, during the call of duty, they and their families were dealt the largest human and material blow.

> وَالَّذِينَ تَبَوَّءُوا الدَّارَ وَالْإِيمَانَ مِن قَبْلِهِمْ يُحِبُّونَ مَنْ هَاجَرَ إِلَيْهِمْ وَلَا يَجِدُونَ فِي صُدُورِهِمْ حَاجَةً مِّمَّا أُوتُوا وَيُؤْثِرُونَ عَلَىٰ أَنفُسِهِمْ وَلَوْ كَانَ بِهِمْ خَصَاصَةٌ ۚ وَمَن يُوقَ شُحَّ نَفْسِهِ فَأُولَٰئِكَ هُمُ الْمُفْلِحُونَ
>
> *Those who were already settled in the abode, and in Īmān (the Anṣār), before they came, love those who have made Hijra to them and do not find in their hearts any need for what they have been given and prefer them to themselves even if they themselves are needy. It is the people who are safe-guarded from the avarice of their own selves who are successful.*[333]

These were the prodigious Anṣār, the greatest instance of civilisation, the sincerest and fullest in their Īmān and the truest to that Īmān by their immense sacrifice and Jihād. Naturally, with such standard and sacrifice, the Anṣār felt excluded during the post-battle distribution at Hunayn.

As such, Saʿd b. ʿUbādah, their leader, was asked to honestly convey their feelings to the Prophet ﷺ. In response, the Messenger delivered them an extraordinary testimony. Giving them no material spoils, he instead expressed realities worth more to the Anṣār than the universe's material treasures combined. He was addressing fertile hearts containing the apex of Īmān and certainty. He asked Saʿd to gather the Anṣār and no one but the Anṣār. Then the noble Messenger ﷺ entered their tent. He thanked Allāh and praised Him. Then, addressing his enduring helpers with the most heartfelt and tender address, he said:

---

[332] *Sīrah* – Ibn Hishām
[333] Al-Qur'ān 59:9

> يا معشر الأنصار، ما قالة، بلغتني عنكم، وجدة وجدتموها علي في أنفسكم؟ ألم آتكم ضلالا فهداكم الله، وعالة فأغناكم الله، وأعداء فألف الله بين قلوبكم .قالوا، بلى، الله ورسوله أمن وأفضل
>
> *"Gathering of Anṣār, what is this you say that has reached me? Is there something you may have found in your hearts against me? Did I not come to you when you were misguided and Allāh guided you, [when you were] poor and Allāh made you rich, [when you were] enemies of one another and Allāh reconciled your hearts?" They answered, "Yes indeed, Allāh and His Messenger are most kind (***Amann** *– most deserving of gratitude) and generous."*

Despite their reality as the helpers, they nonetheless declared favour (*Mann*) as solely belonging to Allāh and His Messenger. Contrast this response to the *Mann* that Banī Asad attributed to themselves. The Messenger ﷺ continued:

> ألا تجيبوني يا معشر الأنصار؟ قالوا، بماذا نجيبك يا رسول الله؟ لله ولرسوله المن والفضل. قال صلى الله عليه وسلم، أما والله لو شئتم لقلتم، فلصدقتم ولصدقتم، أتيتنا مكذبا فصدقناك، ومخذولا فنصرناك، وطريدا فآويناك، وعائلا فآسيناك. أوجدتم يا معشر الأنصار في أنفسكم في لعاعة من الدنيا تألفت بها قوما ليسلموا، ووكلتكم إلى إسلامكم؟ ألا ترضون يا معشر الأنصار أن يذهب الناس بالشاة والبعير، وترجعوا برسول الله إلى رحالكم؟ فوالذي نفس محمد بيده، لولا الهجرة لكنت امرأ من الأنصار، ولو سلك الناس شعبا وسلكت الأنصار شعبا، لسلكت شعب الأنصار. اللهم ارحم الأنصار، وأبناء الأنصار، وأبناء أبناء الأنصار. قال، فبكى القوم حتى أخضلوا لحاهم، وقالوا، رضينا برسول الله قسما، وحظا. ثم انصرف رسول الله صلى الله عليه وسلم، وتفرقوا
>
> *"Why do you not answer me, gathering of Anṣār?" They said, "How shall we answer you Messenger of Allāh? Kindness and generosity (***al-Minna** *– favour) belong to Allāh and His Messenger." He ﷺ said, "Had you by Allāh so wished you could have said – and you would have spoken the truth and been believed – [you could have said], 'you (Messenger) came to us rejected and we believe you (āmannā); deserted and we helped you; a fugitive and we took you in; poor and we comforted you.' Are*

> *you disturbed in mind because of the good things of this life by which I win over a people that they may become Muslims while I entrust you to your Islām?* ***Are you not satisfied that men take away flocks and herds while you take back with you the Messenger of Allāh****? By Him in whose hand is the soul of Muḥammad, if it were not for the migration [from Makkah to Madīnah], I would have been of the Anṣār myself. If everyone went one way and the Anṣār went another, I would take the way of the Anṣār. O Allāh, send Your Mercy on the Anṣār, the children of the Anṣār, and the grandchildren of the Anṣār."*

The entire gathering of the Anṣār wept until tears ran down their beards and they said, *"We are satisfied with the Messenger of Allāh as our lot and portion."*[334] And thus, the fragile newcomers to Islām returned with their flocks and herds, and the Anṣār returned to Madīnah with the Messenger of Allāh ﷺ. And now, gone are the flocks and herds, and the Messenger ﷺ still rests in the land of the Anṣār until the end of time. Was it not a worthy exchange?

Likewise, if we desire only to do the absolute minimum, hoping Islām has a minimum role in our material lives and minimum impact on our worldly fortunes, we have that worldly choice. But then, we cannot expect the position of the Anṣār. The true Mu'minūn are those who strive, conceding certain desires and joys. There are many 'dos' and 'do nots' as a Muslim. Our time, our dress code, our modesty, our earnings, our inner and outer ethics and our relationships are all regulated by Islām. If we feel it becoming burdensome, remember that nothing worthwhile comes without sacrifice. And remember that the greater the sacrifice, the greater the reward.

Some of us will pray and fast during Ramaḍān then as soon as the Ṣalāh or Ramaḍān end, we fly away like birds who were trapped in a cage. Our rushed and unconscious demeanour in ʿIbādah sometimes emerges from the feeling that *'we are doing enough'*, as if Allāh should already be grateful to us. Others may do good, anticipating that they are earning the credit to sin, such as during post-Ramaḍān festivities. This, too, is rooted in the perception of having done Allāh a favour. Our ʿIbādah is our gratitude to Allāh that He allowed us the *privilege* of worshipping Him to begin with. Those after the Battle of Hunayn who gave little took all the herds, flocks, and booty, which in reality is little. Those who gave their souls, their comforts, and their whole lives for Allāh and His Messenger, putting them both *ahead of their own selves*, took with them *exactly that* – their preference of Allāh and His Messenger, above which there is no greater favour. They took with them the master of the children of Ādam who will indeed take them to Paradise.

---

[334] *Musnad* Aḥmad on the authority of Abū Saʿīd al-Khudrī (raḍiy Allāhu ʿanhu)

> فَضْلًا مِّنَ اللَّهِ وَنِعْمَةً ۚ وَاللَّهُ عَلِيمٌ حَكِيمٌ
>
> *It is a great favour from Allāh and a blessing. Allāh is All-Knowing, All-Wise.*[335]

ʿAbdullāh b. Hishām (raḍiy Allāhu ʿanhu) reports that: "*We were with the Prophet ﷺ and he was holding the hand of ʿUmar b. al-Khaṭṭab. ʿUmar said to him*:

> يَا رَسُولَ اللَّهِ لأَنْتَ أَحَبُّ إِلَيَّ مِنْ كُلِّ شَيْءٍ إِلاَّ مِنْ نَفْسِي. فَقَالَ النَّبِيُّ صلى الله عليه وسلم، لاَ وَالَّذِي نَفْسِي بِيَدِهِ حَتَّى أَكُونَ أَحَبَّ إِلَيْكَ مِنْ نَفْسِكَ. فَقَالَ لَهُ عُمَرُ، فَإِنَّهُ الآنَ وَاللَّهِ لأَنْتَ أَحَبُّ إِلَيَّ مِنْ نَفْسِي. فَقَالَ النَّبِيُّ صلى الله عليه وسلم، الآنَ يَا عُمَرُ
>
> *'Allāh's Messenger! You are dearer to me than everything except my own self.' The Prophet ﷺ said, 'No, by Him in Whose Hand my soul is, [you will not have complete Īmān] until I am dearer to you than your own self.' Then 'Umar said to him, 'Now, by Allāh, you are dearer to me than my own self.' The Prophet ﷺ said, 'Now, 'Umar.'*[336] *– meaning now you have attained the completeness of Īmān."*

When to Say 'Āmannā'

Notice that the verse did not chastise the saying, '*we have Īmān*' in general, so as to say '*tell them not to say 'āmannā''*, but rather it affirms, '*lam tu'minū*' (*you do not have Īmān*). Without doubt, Allāh *wants* people to say '*āmannā*', but to say it in truth, with sincerity and after validation, not out of *Mann* or hollowness.[337] Praising the followers of Jesus (ʿĪsā - ʿalayhi al-Salām), Allāh relates that ʿĪsā asked:

> مَنْ أَنصَارِي إِلَى اللَّهِ ۖ قَالَ الْحَوَارِيُّونَ نَحْنُ أَنصَارُ اللَّهِ آمَنَّا بِاللَّهِ وَاشْهَدْ بِأَنَّا مُسْلِمُونَ
>
> *"Who will be my helpers to Allāh?" The disciples said, "We are Allāh's helpers. We have Īmān in Allāh (āmannā billāh). Bear witness that we are Muslims."*[338]

---

[335] Al-Qur'ān 49:8
[336] *Ṣaḥīḥ* Bukhārī on the authority of ʿAbdullāh b. Hishām (raḍiy Allāhu ʿanhu)
[337] *Tafsīr al-Taḥrīr* wa al-Tanwīr – Ibn ʿĀshūr
[338] Al-Qur'ān 61:14

In their case they were honest in their expression and wished to support ʿĪsā (ʿalayhi al-Salām) and so Allāh supported them against those who rejected him. In another verse, Allāh praises the Mu'minūn who:

> الَّذِينَ يَقُولُونَ رَبَّنَا إِنَّنَا آمَنَّا فَاغْفِرْ لَنَا ذُنُوبَنَا وَقِنَا عَذَابَ النَّارِ ۞ الصَّابِرِينَ وَالصَّادِقِينَ وَالْقَانِتِينَ وَالْمُنفِقِينَ وَالْمُسْتَغْفِرِينَ بِالْأَسْحَارِ
>
> *Those* ***who say****, "Our Lord, we have Īmān (āmannā), so forgive us our wrong actions and safeguard us from the punishment of the Fire." [Who are they?] The steadfast, the* ***truthful*** *[in their Īmān, speech, and exteriors], the obedient, the givers, and those who seek forgiveness before dawn.*[339]

[339] Al-Qur'ān 3:16-17

SUMMARISING OUR DISCUSSION

We have taken a brief glimpse from 'Behind the Apartments' into the University of Ethics, Manners and Realities contained in this spectacular *Sūrah* of the Qur'ān. We have attempted to show the interdependence between ethics and Īmān. Īmān is beyond a claim, dress code, or a superficial narrative. It requires earnest effort. It begins with putting Allāh and His Messenger first *in truth*. It involves *truthfully* scrutinising one's *own* desires and inclinations and determining whether they are contrary to the preferences of the Creator, as He and His Messenger ﷺ know best. Such a preference then permeates every level of a nation's political and social structures. The leader is also a subject of Allāh and His Messenger ﷺ, commissioned to dispense the Creator's will on Earth.

A leader must establish firm social justice by systematically maintaining the honour and integrity of the Mu'min. Hearsay and gossip are feeble grounds for drawing judgement against a social order established on Īmān, especially if coming from one with a frail heart and conscience, namely a *Fāsiq*. Were man to impulsively and unjustifiably react to hearsay, assailing his siblings in Īmān, the rest of that community should impulsively reconcile, restoring harmony and mercy in the Prophetic community.

Even if our fellow Mu'min is mistaken, he or she is your own sibling in Īmān, a divinely inspired link that surpasses all other associations. It is a link based on both external and internal convictions and values. Physical conflict cannot be pre-emptively averted, nor can true brotherhood be realised without regulating our external and internal interactions with our siblings. Thus, do not upset your siblings by belittling, offending, or labelling them in their presence. If done in their absence, it is the equivalent of backbiting them, akin to eating their dead flesh. Weed out negative sentiments from the secret depths of your hearts.

Do not suspect evil nor carry out what would develop such sentiments by scrounging for their faults. If one's malice is as a result of suspecting your siblings' inferiority by whatever material judgement one has forged, then know that one's absolute value in the Sight of the King of Kings is by a criterion you cannot perceive. It is by the supreme distinction of *Taqwā* – a covert, classified, and perhaps surprising secret known only to the Knower of the Unseen.

Īmān is both inner and outer and involves a substantiation process through effort and sacrifice. Look at the oldest companions, the Muhājirūn and Anṣār, who surrendered all that they possessed for Allāh and His Messenger ﷺ whilst still acknowledging the favour as being from Allāh, not themselves. They gave up a reviled circumstance of loss and restriction; fatiguing disconnection from their Creator, and derisory social order for the sweetest and most satisfying state of Īmān. It connected them with their Creator and the noblest social order. They are the beneficiaries, but are nonetheless *promised* Paradise. The favour is thus entirely from Allāh and His Messenger ﷺ.

We ask Allāh to accept this small and wholly deficient journey through *al-Ḥujurāt* and to forgive us for our infinite shortfalls. We wrote this work by *His* favour and *Tawfīq*. He inspires His servants to say what He has already clarified and we introduce mistakes of our own. When remembering that we are entirely at the mercy of His strength and utterly in need of His Way, we can only ask for reward humbly and abjectly. He is *al-Raḥmān* and *al-Raḥīm*, worthy of praise and thanks for being so, and thus we say forever, with its true meaning in mind:

Walḥamdu lillāhi rabb al-ʿālamīn.

Printed in Poland
by Amazon Fulfillment
Poland Sp. z o.o., Wrocław

62279788R00096